APPLE IWORK FOR BEGINNERS 2024

3 IN 1

The Most Updated All-in-One
Guide for MAC OS X and iOS Including
Pages, Numbers, and Keynote

ANDREW BLAKE

TABLE OF CONTENTS

PAGES
FOR BEGINNERS

The Most Updated Crash Course to Pages |
Learn How to Create Stunning Documents
in 7 Days or Less

ANDREW BLAKE

INTRODUCTION

Word processing applications have been around for a long time, and nearly everyone who has used a computer since the 1980s has used one. These applications enable you to express yourself verbally, with the white square on your computer screen serving as digital paper to your keyboard's digital ink.

Pages, like Microsoft's Word, fall into the latter category of word processors, which range from the most basic to the most feature-rich. Pages distinguish itself from the rest of the word processor pack through its elegance, ease of use, and simple yet powerful approach to performing tasks that appear to others to be pure drudgery. These features aren't exclusive to Pages in the iWork suite, as Keynote and Numbers have the same beautiful interface and intuitiveness.

You're about to learn just how much simpler being productive is when Apple leads the pack! Apple's iWork suite, which includes Pages, Keynote, and Numbers, approaches word processing, presentations, and spreadsheets in a novel way, and this book will be your guide to getting started with Pages.

This book is intended to introduce you to Apple's approach to performing these tasks, which is (of course) as simple and enjoyable as computer geeks can make them. If you've ever worked with documents, presentations, or spreadsheets, you owe it to yourself to give the iWork suite a try before reverting to your old favorites.

Let's get started.

CHAPTER 1: UNDERSTANDING PAGES

If you're writing a document on your phone, you can open it and continue working on it from your tablet—it's all seamless and doesn't require anything extra on your part once it's set up. You could technically use Pages on a Windows computer, a Chromebook, or an Android device if you set up iCloud because nothing else needs to be installed on your computer; you can even access and edit documents directly in your browser.

When you first use Pages, you'll be given a brief tutorial. You have the option of watching it or skipping it. When you launch Pages, you'll see a directory box asking whether you want to open an existing document or create a new one. We'll create a new document in this chapter, so click "New Document" in the lower left corner. The following box contains all of the templates that are available for use. A template is a pre-made document into which you can insert text. For example, if you want to write a resume, you can use the resume Template and simply keep the formatting while replacing the text that matches you. Templates are organized into categories.

If you don't want to begin with a template, select the first option (which says, Blank). First-time Pages users are frequently disappointed; if you've used Word, you're used to ribbons, menus, and options all over the place! Pages look pretty barren in comparison. Don't worry; appearances can be deceiving; there are plenty of options when you know where to look.

WHAT DO PAGES DO?

Here are some examples of what you can do with Pages at your disposal:

- Easily drop images and other graphics into your documents. You can even align them simply and accurately with little effort, giving your documents an appealing look and feel.
- Share your documents with others easily and quickly, whether they (or you) are on a Mac, using an iPad or iPhone, or on the Web using a non-Mac computer (unfortunately, sometimes it happens) and iCloud.
- Import documents created by Microsoft Word users. You can also export your documents to Word format.
- Get started quickly when creating documents with the beautiful templates included with Pages.
- Using Pages' pre-set styling options, you can instantly change the look and feel of an entire document.
- Create a document. You got it if you want it that simple.
- Take advantage of built-in coaching tips to help guide you in the right direction when you're amidst a feverish word-processing session.
- Make comments and edit documents with uncanny ease.

Become an Internet sensation by writing the next best-selling ebook! (If you're wondering, Pages can export your entire document in ePub format, which is the standard ebook format.)

Pages app may or may not be installed on your Mac, depending on how you obtained it. It is simple to get. Even better, it's completely free!

Pages app is only available as a digital download; no physical copies are available. The file size is a few hundred megabytes.

In the search box, type Pages and press the return key. If you have it, the return result will include an Open button; otherwise, it will include a Get button. You could technically use Pages on a Windows computer, a Chromebook, or an Android device if you set up iCloud because nothing else needs to be installed on your computer; you can even access and edit documents directly in your browser.

The first time you use Pages, you'll get a brief tutorial. You have the option of watching it or skipping it.

When you launch Pages, a directory box will appear and prompt you to choose whether you want to open an existing document or start a new one.

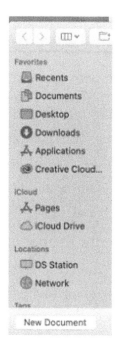

The next box you'll see is all the available templates you can use. A template is a pre-made document to which you can add text into. For example, if you want to write a

resume, you may use the resume template; simply maintain the formatting while replacing the text with your own. Templates are listed under categories.

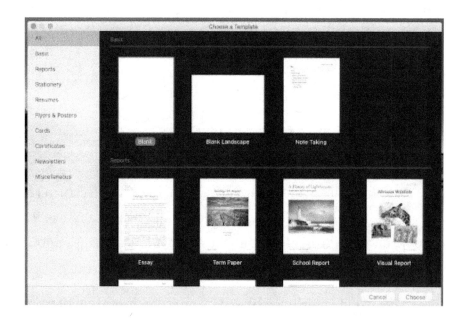

If you don't want to start with a template, then click on the first option (which says, Blank).

First-time Pages users are often disappointed the first time they use Pages; if you've Word, then you have ribbons and menus and options everywhere! Pages look pretty bare next to that.

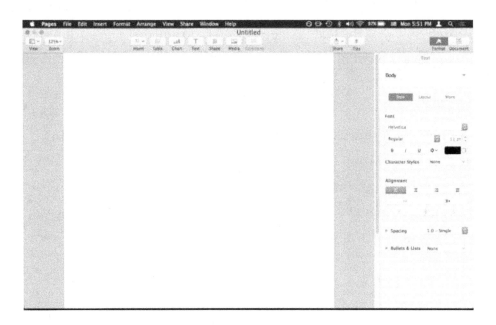

Don't worry—looks can be deceiving; there are plenty of options when you know

how to find them, and I'll show you each in this book. You can conceal the side panel by clicking the Format icon in the top right corner if you already feel overwhelmed by the options.

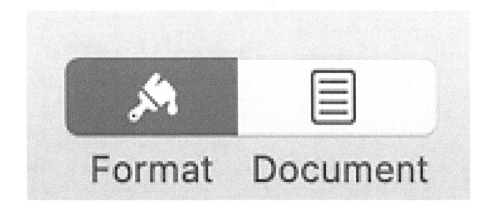

Now that you have a blank screen let's go over the very basics of Pages.

- **Select:** To select a single word, move your mouse over it and click twice.
- **Select Paragraph:** To select all words in the paragraph, click three times over any word in the paragraph you want to select.

- **Select All:** Selecting All means selecting everything in your document. It's a very strong command! It displays the same options as Select, but any changes you make will be reflected throughout the document. To Select All, use the command + A on your keyboard.

- **Select Options:** Now that the text is selected, what do you do? The options box comes up if you click with two fingers on your trackpad or mouse. We'll review these options as we continue in the book.

- **Cut, Copy and Paste:** To copy and paste words (as well as images, tables, and charts) quicker, you can use keyboard shortcuts. Selecting content and hitting COMMAND + C will copy it. Selecting content and hitting COMMAND + X will cut it. And hitting COMMAND + V will copy the content anywhere you want it in the document.

- **Find and Replace:** Pages has a handy feature called Find and Replace that allows you to replace your selection with alternatives. It only takes a few seconds! Go to edit from your menu bar and select Find.

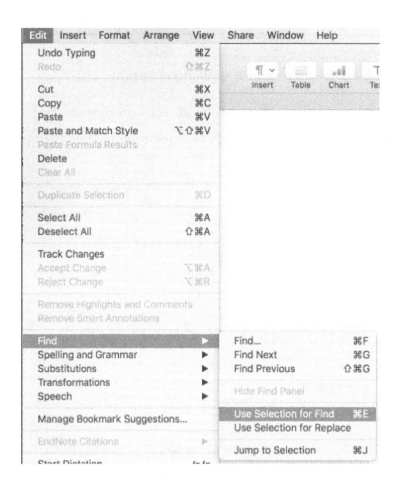

The term you're looking for will be found here in all instances, but by selecting the down arrow on the left side, you can also choose Find & Replace. With this, you can look up a term (top line) and replace it when it turns up (bottom line). When you have both the find and replace Word added, you can click Replace & Find.

- **Define:** Pages include a handy little dictionary. To see the definition of any word, select it, click the trackpad twice to bring up the options menu, and then tap Look Up.

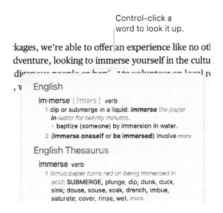

The dictionary will give you multiple definitions (and a thesaurus); even more, you can select options at the bottom to see movies related to the Word, Siri Knowledge (which is encyclopedic information), apps related to it, and more!

- **Copy Style:** The Style command, like the Microsoft Word format painter feature, allows you to copy and paste styles. If you want to make one piece of text look like another, select the text with the format you wish to copy and then click Copy. Click Format > Copy Style; select the text you want to change, and click Format > Paste Style. This can be a major time saver!

- **Inserting Hyperlinks:** Simply type out the link to insert a hyperlink to an internet resource. Pages automatically detect hyperlinks and will insert the link for you. Click the link and tap Link Settings to edit the link or change the displayed text. Here you can edit the link itself, change the text displayed, or remove the link altogether.

If you aren't typing a web address but want to link it to one (for example, "I go to UCLA" and provide a hyperlink to UCLA), select the Word you wish to hyperlink and click with two fingers to bring up the options. Simply click Add Link and choose the type of link you want to add. You can edit and delete it in the same way that you did in the previous paragraph.

- **Undo/Redo:** If you make a mistake (for example, accidentally delete a paragraph), you can undo it by going to Edit > Undo; you can also redo it from the same menu.
- **The Formatting Toolbar:** There are a few menu options to work with in Pages, but in this section, we will cover the Formatting Toolbar, which is on the right side of your document.

Under the text, it will say "Body" by default. When you click it, you'll see several options. "Body" is normal text in a document—the text you are reading here would be considered Body Text. Documents have several types of paragraph text; you could just change the font size and make it "look" like a heading, but using a Paragraph Style tells Pages what kind of text it is so it can put together a table of contents later. Some styles will not be very common, "Label Dark," for example.

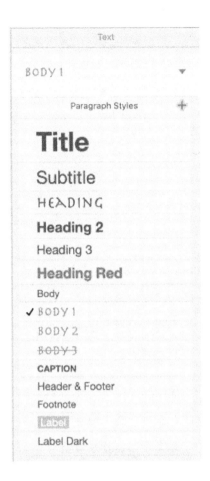

Under this are options for Style, Layout, and More. Let's stay on style now, so the next option is font. It says 11pt Helvetica; this is the font. If you tap on it, you'll be able to change the font and size. Pages offers a healthy font selection, including perennial favorites like Arial, Times New Roman, and Helvetica. Some notable absences include Comic Sans (yet Papyrus still made the cut), Calibri, and Cambria.

The "regular" drop-down shows you all the style choices for that font (some fonts have different options).

1. The next three buttons are pretty standard. If you're unfamiliar with computerized word processing, remember B for Bold, I for Italic, and U for underline. The S with a line through it inserts a strikethrough into any text you type.

2. Your alignment buttons are located beneath this. Tap them to align or justify your text to the left, center, or right. Justified text fills exactly one line. You can play around with these different alignment options to see how it works.

3. The next two buttons are indent buttons. They can be used to indent or to move backward through indents. Finally, you can add bulleted lists and line spacing below this (if you want to double-space, for example).

- **Layout:** Text can be placed in columns, and line spacing can be adjusted using the Layout menu. You can use Pages to write that paper for your picky professor who requires 1.25 spacing (click indents)! Columns can also be created using layout (if you are writing a newsletter, for example).

OPENING PAGES FROM ICLOUD

Pages can be run right from your browser; it's great for editing, but for intensive design work, the best solution will be your computer. To access it from your browser, head to iCloud.com and sign in with your Apple ID.

The first screen will show you all the things you can do from the cloud; one of them is using Pages. Click it once to open it.

As long as you've been saving your work to the cloud, any recent documents will appear here, and you can open them by clicking on their thumbnail once. You can also create a new document by clicking the + button in the upper right corner. This will launch iCloud Pages. The features discussed in this book are also available in Pages for iCloud.

MANAGING DOCUMENTS

To manage documents, there are several options available on pages beyond simply saving a document using the "File > Save" command.

Here are some examples of how to manage your Pages documents:

1. Save As: To create a copy of your document with a different name or file format, use "File > Save As." This option is particularly useful if you want to create a new version of a document without overwriting the original file.

2. Versions: Pages allow you to save versions of your document, which can be accessed by selecting "File > Revert To >Browse All Versions." This feature lets you go back to an earlier version of your document if needed or compare different versions side-by-side.

3. iCloud: Pages integrate with iCloud, Apple's cloud storage service, allowing you to save your documents to the cloud and access them from any device with an internet connection. To save a document to iCloud, simply select "File > Save to iCloud."

4. Export: Pages allow you to export your document to a variety of file formats, including Word, PDF, and ePub. To do this, select "File > Export to" and choose the desired file format from the list.

5. Share: If you need to share your document with others, Pages provides several sharing options. You can use "File > Share" to share your document via email, Messages, or AirDrop, or choose "File > Collaborate" to collaborate with others on the same document in real time.

PAGES BASICS

Pages is a word processing and desktop publishing application that is a part of the iWork suite of apps. It is designed for macOS, iPad, and iOS devices and offers a range of features to help users create and format text documents.

The Pages interface is user-friendly, and users can customize their preferences to work the way they want. The app has a toolbar that provides easy access to frequently used tools such as font styles, paragraph formatting, and page layout options. The sidebar offers quick access to document components such as table of contents, bookmarks, and comments. Additionally, Pages has a wide range of templates and themes that users can choose from to make their documents more visually appealing.

With Pages, users can add, edit, and format text in a variety of ways. Users can choose from a range of fonts and font styles, adjust the size and color of text, and add various formatting options such as bold, italics, underline, and strikethrough. Pages also allow users to create and modify tables, add images and media, and use graphics tools to create shapes, lines, and charts.

In addition to working with text, Pages allows users to work with different parts of their documents, such as headers, footers, and styles. Users can create a consistent look and feel throughout their document by using templates and themes, applying styles to text, and creating and modifying headers and footers. Pages also offer a range of page layout options, including margins, page size, and orientation, which users can adjust to suit their needs.

While Pages may not have every function that some other word processors do, it offers a unique user experience that prioritizes usability over having every possible tool at the user's disposal. Pages app is designed to be simple and easy to use while still providing users with the ability to create high-quality documents.

Ultimately, the choice of which word processor to use comes down to personal preference and necessity. Some users may prioritize having every possible tool at their disposal, while others may prefer a simpler, more user-friendly experience. Regardless of which camp you fall into, the Pages app is a powerful tool for creating and formatting text documents that can help you create beautiful and professional-looking documents.

CONFIGURING PAGE PREFERENCES

Each of us has our personality and way of doing things. Even though Apple would prefer that we do everything their way, they allow us some leeway as individual users with some of the options in Pages. These options are known as preferences, and I'll show you how to set them in each version of Pages.

Preferences for OS X

To access the preferences in Pages on macOS, follow these steps:

1. Open Pages.
2. Click on "Pages" in the menu bar at the top of the screen.
3. Click on "Preferences."

Alternatively, you can use the keyboard shortcut Command (⌘) + Comma (,).

When you open the Preferences window, you can select from several tabs, including "General," "Rulers," and "Auto-Correction."

The Template Chooser is no longer a part of Pages. Instead, Pages now includes a "Document Manager" that allows you to choose from a variety of templates, including Blank, Basic, and more. To access the Document Manager, follow these steps:

1. Open Pages.
2. Click on "File" in the menu bar at the top of the screen.
3. Click on "New."
4. In the Document Manager, choose the template that you want to use.

Proofreading

To access the proofreading preferences in Pages, follow these steps:

1. Open Pages.
2. Click on "Pages" in the menu bar at the top of the screen.
3. Click on "Preferences."
4. Click on the "Proofreading" tab.

In the Proofreading tab, you can configure the default actions for editing a document. Here's a summary of the available options:

- Check Spelling: Check this box to enable automatic spell-checking as you type.
- Correct Spelling Automatically: Check this box to allow Pages to automatically correct spelling mistakes as you type.
- Detect lists automatically: Check this box to enable automatic list formatting when Pages detect a list in your document.
- Show Substitutions: Check this box to enable automatic substitutions, such as replacing double hyphens with an em dash (—) or replacing straight quotes with smart quotes.
- Show Spelling and Grammar: Check this box to enable the spelling and grammar check as you type.
- Show Predictive: Check this box to enable the predictive text feature, which suggests words as you type.
- Author: Enter a name to be used when tracking changes and adding comments to a document.

Note: There is no option to configure Bézier curves or show invisible elements in the Proofreading tab of Pages. The option to optimize movies for iOS devices is now located in the Document tab under "Movie Playback" instead of the Proofreading tab.

Rulers Tab

To access the Rulers preferences in Pages, follow these steps:

1. Open Pages.
2. Click on "Pages" in the menu bar at the top of the screen.
3. Click on "Preferences."
4. Click on the "Rulers" tab.

In the Rulers tab, you can configure options that assist you in deciding where to place items in your document. Here's a summary of the available options:

- Ruler Units: Select a default unit of measurement from the pop-up menu.
- Show size and position on move: Check this box to see an on-screen prompt showing the size and position of an object as you move it within the document.
- Enable vertical ruler: Check this box to display a vertical ruler on the left side of the document window when the horizontal ruler is displayed. This can be useful when working with documents that contain body text.
- Alignment guides: Check this box to enable alignment guides that help you correctly place an object within the document's boundaries and among other objects. You can specify the color of the alignment guides and choose to show them at the center and/or edges of objects.

CHAPTER 2: DOCUMENT SETUP USING PAGES

For most documents, the pre-set template will suffice; for those who require a bit more customization, there is Document Setup (similar to Page Setup in Word); here, you can adjust margins, headers, and footers.

DOCUMENT CONFIGURATION

Here is a step-by-step guide on how to access Document Setup in Pages.

1. Open Pages on your Mac device.
2. If you don't see the sidebar, click on the "View" menu in the menu bar and select "Show Sidebar."
3. In the sidebar, click on the "Document" tab, which is the first tab on the left. You can also use the keyboard shortcut Command+Option+P to open Document Setup.

4. In the Document tab, you can configure the settings for your document, including page orientation, size, and margins. You can also enable facing pages, adjust the document background, and set up headers and footers.

5. To switch to the Sections or Bookmarks tabs, simply click on the corresponding icon in the sidebar.

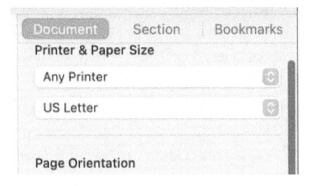

6. In the Sections tab, you can add, delete, and modify sections within your document.

7. In the Bookmarks tab, you can add bookmarks to specific sections of your document for easy navigation.

CHANGING THE MARGINS AND SIZE OF A DOCUMENT

To change the margins and size of a document in Pages version 12.2.1, follow these steps:

1. In the sidebar, click on the "Document" tab, which is the first tab on the left. You can also use the keyboard shortcut Command+Option+P to open Document Setup.
2. In the Document tab, you can configure the settings for your document, including page orientation, size, and margins.
3. To change the size of your document, click on the drop-down menu next to "Page Size" and select the size you want. You can also create a custom size by selecting "Custom" and entering the dimensions you want.
4. To change the margins of your document, click on the drop-down menu next to "Margins" and select the margin size you want. You can also create custom margins by selecting "Custom" and entering the margin measurements you want.
5. If you want to enable facing pages, click on the checkbox next to "Facing Pages." This will allow you to see a two-page spread on your screen and print your document as a booklet.
6. When you're done making changes, click "OK" to save your document settings.

MAKING YOUR PAPER SIZE

What if your size isn't listed? You can make a custom size, but remember that it may not print correctly if you print the document. Go to File > Page Setup to create a custom size. Then, under Paper Size, select a size from the drop-down menu. Finally, enter your customized size.

LIGATURES AND HYPHENATIONS

There are two checkboxes at the bottom of Document Setup: Hyphenations and Ligatures. Checking them toggles their status. Ligatures and hyphenations are typographic features that are used in text documents to improve readability and visual appearance.

A ligature is a single glyph that is created by combining two or more letters or characters. This is done to improve the spacing and readability of text. For example, the letters "f" and "i" in the word "life" can be joined together to form a ligature, which is a single glyph that looks like a connected "fi." Ligatures can also be used for other combinations of letters, such as "ff," "fl," and "ffi."

Hyphenation, on the other hand, is the process of dividing a word at the end of a line so that part of the Word appears on the next line. Hyphenation is used to prevent large gaps or awkward spacing between words in justified text. When a word is hyphenated, a hyphen is placed at the end of the line, and the rest of the Word is moved to the next line. Hyphenation can be automatic or manual, depending on the preferences set by the user.

PAGE NUMBERS AND HEADERS

The header and footer options in Document Setup Mode are extremely useful. These document elements will be visible on all pages of your document. You'll be able to add page numbers from here as well. In the Document section of Setup, you can change the size of the Header and Footer. The section determines where the Header and Footer appear. The section allows you to instruct Pages not to include your Header/Footer on your title page or to begin numbering on a specific page. Simply move your cursor to the top of the page, and you'll see a table with three cells representing left, right, and center alignment. You will also be able to add the page number to any of these cells.

BOOKMARKS

Bookmarks are ideal for electronic documents. When you add a bookmark, it is indexed, and you can later hyperlink to it. So, for example, you could be on page 2 of a 500-page document and have it refer to a bookmark on page 87; when the user clicks it, it jumps to the section marked. To make one, highlight the text you want to bookmark, navigate to the Bookmark tab of Document Setup, and click the Add Bookmark button. Whatever text you highlight is automatically named as a bookmark. So, if the highlighted text says, "This is a bookmark," the bookmark is called "This is a bookmark." You can single-click the name and rename it. This will only change the bookmark's name, not the text itself.

To add bookmarks to your document, follow these steps:

1. Open Pages on your Mac device.
2. Open the document you want to work with.
3. Scroll to the location in your document where you want to add a bookmark.
4. Click on the "Insert" menu in the menu bar and select "Bookmark."
5. In the Bookmark panel, you can give your bookmark a name and choose whether to include the bookmark in the table of contents. You can also assign a keyboard shortcut to your bookmark.
6. Click "Add" to add your bookmark to your document.
7. To navigate to a bookmark in your document, click on the "View" menu in the menu bar and select "Go To" > "Bookmark." This will open the Bookmark panel, where you can select the bookmark you want to go to and click "Go To" to navigate to that location.
8. If you want to edit or delete a bookmark, click on the "Bookmark" menu in the menu bar and select "Edit Bookmarks." This will open the Bookmark panel, where you can select the bookmark you want to edit or delete and make changes as needed.

TABLE OF CONTENTS

If you are working on a document that requires a table of contents, you must first ensure that you use the correct headings. Headings inform Pages about what will appear in the table of contents. To make a heading, highlight the text you want to be the heading, then go to the format sidebar.

You can change how the heading is formatted by clicking the arrow next to it; for example, if you want your heading to match the formatting you have, simply click Redefine from Selection.

Once you've completed all of the headings in the document, go to Insert > Table of Contents and select the type you want. The most common is the document. If you click on the inserted table of contents, a table of contents format will appear in the format options in the right pane of Pages; here, you can choose what you want to appear in your table of contents. Uncheck everything else, for example, if you only want Heading 1 to appear.

FOOTNOTES

To insert a footnote into your document, select Insert > Footnote after selecting the text to which you want to add a footnote. In chapter 4, you will learn in detail about footnotes.

ADD A COMMENT

To add a comment in Pages for Mac:

1. Select the text or object you want to comment on.
2. Click on "Insert" in the top menu, then click on "Comment."
3. Alternatively, you can use the shortcut Command + Option + M to insert a comment.
4. Type your comment in the text box that appears in the right sidebar.
5. Click outside the comment box to close it.

To add a comment in Pages for iOS:

1. Select the text or object you want to comment on by tapping and holding it.
2. Tap "Comment" in the pop-up menu.
3. Type your comment in the text box that appears at the bottom of the screen.
4. Tap "Done" to close the comment box.

MONITOR CHANGES

When editing a document, it's also a good idea to enable Track Changes, which allows the other person to see what you've changed. Track changes are enabled under Edit > Track Changes (and deactivated in the exact location). When enabled, a new bar appears at the document's top, and the changed text's color changes. The user must now accept or reject changes to the document; if they reject them, the changes are removed.

SHARING AND EXPORTING DOCUMENTS

Despite the popularity of iPhones and iPads, Apple users are frequently stranded in a Windows-based world. Pages is an excellent program but incomprehensible to Microsoft Word users. Fortunately, Pages provides several methods for sharing and exporting documents in various formats. Pages also make document sharing between Apple devices a breeze, thanks to iCloud.

USING ICLOUD TO SYNC DOCUMENTS

If you've enabled iCloud in your Pages app, your documents will automatically sync across all your devices with no effort. You can also access your documents online at www.i-cloud.com from any internet connection.

EMAILING A DOCUMENT

From Pages Emailing documents is one of the simplest ways to share your document. Navigate to Share > Send a Copy.

COLLABORATING

You can also work on a document by going to Share > Collaborate With Others. This displays an option that asks how you want to share the document. I recommend selecting the Share Options drop-down menu to ensure that the appropriate permissions are enabled. You can, for example, make the document readable to anyone you share it with or who receives it; you can also grant the user the ability to make changes.

PAGES DOCUMENT EXPORT

By default, your file will be saved as a Pages document. That's fine if you have Pages, but if you want to share it with (or open it on) a computer that doesn't have Pages, or if you want to create a universal PDF that anyone can view, you'll need to export it. This is relatively simple. Navigate to File > Export. There are six types of files:

- PDF

- Word
- EPUB
- Plain Text Format
- Rich Text Format
- Pages'09

If you want to keep all the formatting in the document and have it look exactly like it does in Pages, PDF is the best option. Plain text will remove all formatting but be readable in almost any editor. If you want to create an eBook of your document that can be opened in something like iBooks, you will use ePub. Some eReaders do not open ePubs natively and will convert them, so formatting may be lost.

Printing Go to File > Print to print a document. There's also a PDF save option at the bottom of the print menu—pages equivalent to Print to File.

CREATING NEW DOCUMENTS

It doesn't get any simpler than creating new documents, and it's simple in all three versions. To make a new document in Pages, follow these steps:

- In OS X, select File > New or press N to access the Template Chooser. Choose a template for your new document by clicking the Choose button in the lower right corner.
- iOS Tap the Create Document icon to open the Template Chooser from within the Documents manager (if you're already in a document, simply tap Documents in the upper left corner to get to this screen). The template you want to use will open automatically after you tap it.
- iCloud Open the Template Chooser by clicking the Create Document icon on the iCloud Pages screen.

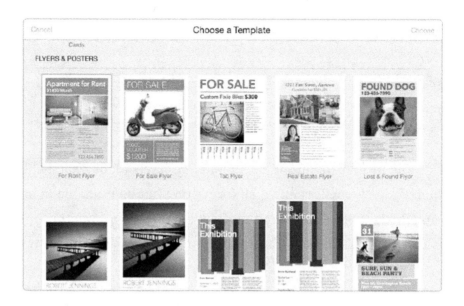

DOCUMENT SAVING AND RENAMING

Typically, creating documents without saving them is a massive waste of time, but that's just one man's opinion, right? So, for those readers who share my sentiments, let's see how we can go about saving our creations. We'll also look at how to rename documents while we're at it.

- For OS X, press S or select File > Save to save a document. The Save As window will appear if you are saving this document for the first time. Simply give the document a title, select a location for it, and click the Save button. To rename a document, select File > Rename, type the new name (the document title in the middle of the window will be highlighted blue, in case you're wondering where your changes are showing), and press RETURN; your document has now been renamed.

- For iOS, Pages automatically saves your documents, but it doesn't give them names other than "Blank" or "Blank 2," so you'll be grateful for the ability to easily rename documents. Tap the name of the document you want to rename in the Documents manager. Enter the name of your document in the Rename Document field and press the Done button on the keyboard.

- Pages for iCloud save your documents automatically, but like iOS, you start with names like "Blank." Fortunately, renaming the new document is just as simple. Open the Documents manager, select the name of the document to rename, type the name in the provided field, and press RETURN.

It is very simple to rename documents. There is more than one way to do it in Pages, as with many other things. When your document is open, simply click on the name in the top center of the document.

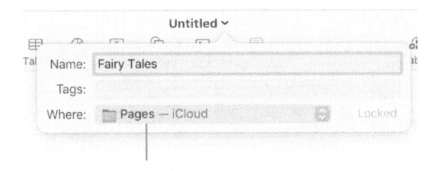

The next way is File > Rename.

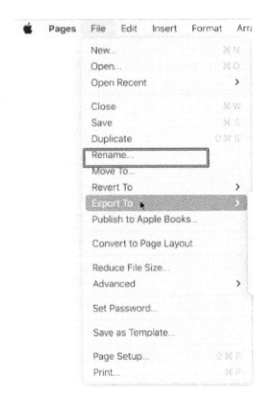

The third way is to find it in Finder, click with two fingers, and select Rename.

Exercise: Open up a blank Pages document. Copy and paste a chunk of text from somewhere else.

Hint: you can visit a webpage and copy text the same way in Pages. Then, go back to Pages and paste. Format it to display as 14 pt., justified, bold, double-spaced red Arial. Format your text so that it is shown in three columns. (Remember Columns is under the layout.)

OPENING EXISTING FILES

It is simple to create new documents, as well as to open existing ones. OS X It is very simple to open documents stored in iCloud or on your Mac:

1. Press O or select File > Open.
2. In the upper left corner of the window, choose iCloud or On My Mac, depending on where the document is saved.
3. Double-click the document you want to open, then click the Open button in the window's lower right corner. Of course, you can skip the last small step by double-clicking a document within the window.

iCloud and iOS Opening an existing document are the same for both the iOS and iCloud versions of Pages. Simply open the Documents manager and select the document you want to open (in iCloud, you must double-click the document).

PASSWORDS AND DOCUMENT LOCKING

Some people take security very seriously, and Pages allows those who want to keep their little secrets to themselves. One option is to use a password to prevent those who do not know it from changing a document, and another is to lock a document to prevent any tinkering.

A password is a secure way to protect your document from prying eyes and others who might inadvertently change its contents. Once a password has been assigned to a document, no one can open it, let alone change it, unless they know the password.

To give a document a password, do the following:

*   For OS X: To open the password dialog, select File > Set Password. Enter the password in the Password and Verify fields, and optionally enter a hint in the Password Hint field before clicking the Set Password button.
*   For iOS: Open the document, then select Tools > Set Password. Enter the password in the Password and Verify fields, optionally enter a hint in the Password Hint field (Apple recommends it, but I don't), and then tap the Go button on the on-screen keyboard (or Done in the upper right corner of the window).
*   For Apple iCloud: Open the document, click the Tools icon, then Set Password. Enter the password in the Password and Verify fields, optionally enter a hint in the Password Hint field (Apple recommends it, but I don't), and then click the Set Password button. Simply type the

password when prompted to open a password-protected document. You're out of luck, my friend if you don't know the password.

Locking a document prevents anyone from editing, renaming, moving, or deleting it. However, keep in mind that locking a document is only available in the OS X version of Pages. To secure a document:

1. Move the mouse pointer over the document's title (which must be open in Pages to be locked) until you see a small gray arrow next to it; click the gray arrow.
2. To lock the document, check the Locked box. To return to the document, click outside the window. When you try to change a document element, you will be reminded that it is locked.

ORGANIZING PAGES AND DOCUMENTS

When editing a document, keep track of the changes. Text search and replacement Check your spelling and make use of autocorrect. Make use of the built-in reference tools. Make comments and highlight text. Adding text to a document and embellishing it with images and graphics is only one aspect of document creation. Now comes the fun part: editing, proofreading, and ensuring you've got everything in order before making your document available for public consumption.

A document intended for public consumption is frequently subjected to extensive editing, whether by the person who created the document or by several other interested parties such as copy editors, technical editors, and so on (you all know who you are).

While getting feedback from multiple sources is beneficial and can result in a more polished final product, not knowing who is saying what in the editorial comments can be unsettling, not to mention all manner of higgledy-piggledy.

Pages' tracking changes feature can display changes and comments made by your document's other beneficiaries in an orderly fashion, allowing you to sift through the mountain of editing information. When you enable Track Changes, the changed text appears in a different color than the rest of the text in the document, and a change bar appears in the document's margin.

TRANSFERRING DOCUMENTS TO AND FROM ICLOUD

Moving your documents to iCloud makes them available to you and others from any computer or iOS device that can connect to the Internet. As you might expect, removing documents from iCloud has the opposite effect. Unfortunately, this handy little trick is only available in the OS X version of Pages. To transfer a document from your computer to iCloud, follow these steps:

1. Select File > Move To.
2. From the pop-up menu, choose a location. If you don't see the location you're looking for in the menu, select Other at the bottom to browse your hard drive.
3. Select the Move option. Your document will be physically moved from its previous location to the one you specify rather than copied.

USING ICLOUD TO SHARE DOCUMENTS

Pages enable you to share a document with anyone by sending them a link to the document in iCloud.

When you share a document via iCloud, you send a web link to the document's location within iCloud, as previously stated. Anyone with Pages (on a Mac, an iOS device, or a Windows PC using iCloud) can open (and Edit) the document by clicking the link. Any changes they make to the document will be saved. This system can be either the pinnacle of collaboration or disaster; did you remember password-protecting your document? The links can be sent via email, Messages, Twitter, Facebook, or any other method you can think of to reach your intended recipient.

To share a document from OS X Pages via iCloud, follow these steps:

1. Launch the document that you want to share. It is recommended that the document be password protected.
2. In the toolbar, click the Share button.
3. Using the Share Link Via iCloud context menu, select the method you want to use to share the iCloud link to your document.

SHARING A DOCUMENT LINK FROM THE MAIL APP IN OS X

Examine the Share icon in the toolbar once the link has been sent to the recipient. You'll notice that it's changed from a white box with an upward arrow to a group of strangely colored people. Those green goblins are simply informing you that the document has been distributed. When in shared mode, click the Share button to do the following:

- Using the Change Password button, change the password for the document.
- Click the Stop Sharing button to stop sharing the document.
- Send the link to someone else by selecting a method from the pop-up menu and clicking the Send Link button.
- Hold your mouse pointer over the link until you see a gray button labeled Copy Link. Click it to copy the link to your Mac's clipboard, and then paste it into any document or sharing mechanism you deem appropriate.

To share a document via iCloud from iOS, follow these steps:

1. Launch the document that you want to share. It is recommended that the document be password protected!
2. In the toolbar, tap the Share button.
3. Select the option to Share Link Via iCloud. Choose how you want to distribute the iCloud link to your document. You'll notice that AirDrop is yet another sharing method that can be used from an iOS device to share the link with other iOS devices.

The Share icon has been changed to our green guys, as in the OS X version of Pages. When in shared mode, tap the Share button to do the following:

- Change the document's password by tapping Change password.
- Stop sharing the document by selecting Stop Sharing.
- Tap Send a link and choose a method from the pop-up menu to send the link to someone else.
- Tap the link to bring up a dark gray button labeled Copy. Tap the Copy button to copy the link to your device's clipboard, and then paste it into any document or sharing mechanism you prefer.

To share a document via iCloud from within Pages for iCloud, follow these steps:

1. Launch the document that you want to share. Again, if the document isn't already password-protected, it should be.
2. In the toolbar, click the Share button, then the blue Share Document button.
3. A window appears stating, "This document is shared." You can do the following from within this window:

- Using the Change Password button, change the password for the document.
- Click the Stop Sharing button to stop sharing the document.
- Click the Email Link button in the iCloud Mail app to send the link to someone else.
- Highlight the link by pressing C (Mac) or CONTROL-C (PC), then copy the link to your computer's clipboard and paste it into any document or sharing mechanism you need to use. To return to the "This document is shared" window, click the Share button in the toolbar (those green people again), followed by Settings.

PAGES EXPORTING FILES

Pages is similar to a Swiss Army knife in that it can export files to various formats, allowing them to be viewed and worked with in other apps.

To export a document from Pages for Mac:

1. If it isn't already open, open the document you want to export.
2. Go to the File menu and hover your mouse over the Export To menu.
3. Choose the format in which you want to save your file.
4. When the Export Your Document window appears, make any necessary selections based on your exporting format.

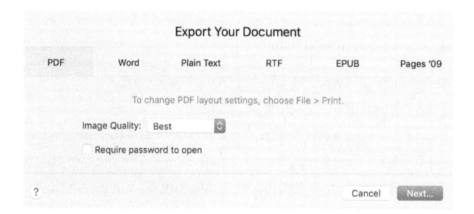

5. Select Next.
6. Select a location to save your new file, rename it if desired, and click Export to finish the process.

Pages for iCloud allows you to export a document in two ways: from within an open document and from within the Documents manager. We'll take a look at both now. To export from an open document, do the following:

1. Navigate to Tools > Download A Copy.
2. Choose the format in which you want to save your file.
3. When Pages is done formatting the document, it will download to your browser's default downloads folder.

To export from the Documents manager:

1. Click once on the document you want to export to highlight it.
2. At the top of the window, click the Document And Sort Options button (it looks like a gear) and select Download Document from the menu.
3. Select the format to which you want to export your file.
4. When Pages is done formatting the document, it will download to your browser's default downloads folder.

ADDING FILES TO PAGES

Pages support non-native file formats such as Pages '09, Word, PDF, ePub, and Plain Text. As previously stated, importing a file into Pages is as simple as opening it, which in OS X is the same as opening any other file:

1. Press O or select File > Open.
2. In the upper left corner of the window, choose iCloud or On My Mac, depending on where the document is saved.

To open a document, click on it and then click the Open button in the window's lower right corner. You can also open a document by double-clicking it within the window. However, you must first load a file into Pages for iOS and Pages for iCloud before they can attempt to open it, which brings us back to our discussion of transferring files with iTunes.

USING ITUNES TO TRANSFER FILES TO AND FROM PAGES

iTunes is everyone's favorite digital music and video store, jukebox, and tool for syncing our iOS devices with our computers. Still, it can also transfer files to and from Pages on iOS devices. This tip is especially useful if you don't use or have access to iCloud but still need to work on your documents on a computer. To transfer files from iTunes to Pages for iOS, follow these steps:

1. Connect your iOS device to your computer and launch iTunes.
2. Once it appears, select your device in iTunes (it will appear in the upper right corner of the window).
3. Select Apps from the toolbar at the top of the window, then scroll to the bottom.
4. Select Pages from the File Sharing Apps list.
5. Click the Add button in the lower right and then navigate to the file you want to transfer on your computer. When you've found it, select it and then click Add.
6. Navigate to Pages on your iOS device.
7. Navigate to the Documents manager and click the + icon in the upper left corner; then select Copy From iTunes.

When the Copy From iTunes window appears, tap the name of the file you want to transfer to Pages on your iOS device. When the transfer is finished, the document will be added to the Documents manager and can be opened with a single tap.

To transfer files from Pages for iOS to iTunes, follow these steps:

1. Connect your iOS device to your computer and launch iTunes (not the iOS device).
2. Once it appears, select your device in iTunes (it will appear in the upper right corner of the window).
3. Select Apps from the toolbar at the top of the window, then scroll to the bottom.
4. Select Pages from the File Sharing Apps list.
5. Launch Pages on your iOS device and perform one of the following actions:
   - If the document to be transferred is not open, tap the Share button in the upper left corner of the screen (it looks like a square with an upward-pointing arrow) and choose to Send A Copy from the menu. To highlight the document you want to transfer, tap it.
   - While working on the document you want to transfer, tap the Share button in the upper right corner of the screen and choose to Send A Copy from the menu.
5. Open the Send To iTunes window by tapping the iTunes icon.
8. Select the file format for which you want to save the document. The document will appear in iTunes' Pages Documents list when the transfer is finished. Select the file, then click the Save To button in the lower right, navigate to a location on your computer, and click the Save To button.

Remember the "paperless office" fantasy we once had? Even the most die-hard digital fanatics would agree that we're still far from that. To be honest, I like having a little paper in my office because it keeps me from forgetting that I still have work to do. Printing documents from Pages is fairly simple, so let's get started, shall we? OS X To print documents from Pages for OS X, follow these steps:

1. Open the Page Setup sheet by pressing SHIFT-P or selecting File > Page Setup, and then do the following:
    a. In the Format menu, select the printer you want to send your document for printing.
    b. Choose the appropriate Paper Size, Orientation, and Scale options, then click OK.
2. To open the Print dialog sheet, press P or select File > Print, and then do the following:
    a. In the Printer pop-up menu, select the printer to which you want to send the print job.
    b. Make any additional choices, such as the number of copies to print or whether to print two-sided (if your printer supports such a feature).
3. To send your job to the printer, click the Print button in the lower right corner.

Printing from Pages in iOS is even simpler because there aren't many options to play with (it's pretty much print and be done).

To print from Pages in iOS, follow these steps:

1. Open the document to be printed.
2. Tap the Tools icon in the upper right corner, then select Print from the menu.
3. If the printer you require isn't already selected, tap Select Printer. Explore the available printers and tap to choose the one you want to use.
4. Determine how many copies of the document you want to print and press the + or - button to the right.
5. Select the Print option to send your job on its way. iCloud Printing from Pages for iCloud differs from printing from Pages for OS X or iOS in that Pages for iCloud can only print PDFs. Furthermore, the PDFs generated by Pages will print from your browser or your computer's default PDF application rather than directly from Pages.

To print from iCloud:

1. Launch the document you want to print.
2. Select Print from the Tools menu in the upper right corner.
3. Pages will create a PDF version of your document. When the PDF is ready, click the Open PDF button to open it in your browser or your preferred PDF application.
4. Print normally from your browser or a PDF app.

CHAPTER 3: WORKING WITH TEMPLATES IN PAGES

Pages for iPad includes over 50 templates divided into ten categories, including some for letters, others for reports and professional use, and others for personal correspondence and announcements.

A Template is a pre-formatted document that includes text and images. What would make you want that? The idea is to delete the text (and replace the images) to personalize it while saving time on the sometimes complicated formatting. Try "Classic Letter" or "Formal Letter" if you need a standard business letter. You can also try the Personal and Modern Photo letters for a more unusual, offbeat look. Some templates have multiple pages, such as a "splashy" front page with enough space for a large photo, followed by more subdued pages with details. This category includes the majority of academic and business-related style templates. "Project Proposal," "Term Paper," and "Visual Report" are all excellent places to begin a highly visual educational or proposal project. Pages also have party invitations, thank you cards, and recipe formats. You can use any of these templates as a starting point now that you understand most formatting options in Pages. Each template's images, colors, and layout can be customized to meet the requirements of your project.

Pages' way of assisting in creating new documents is through templates. They are pre-built documents of various types, so all you have to do is plug in your specific information rather than start from scratch. You can either use the templates provided by Apple or create your templates, whichever suits your fancy at the time.

UTILIZING PRE-EXISTING TEMPLATES

Each Pages version has its templates to help you start creating new documents. These templates are available in the Template Chooser, which is easily accessible and simple. Browse through the various template categories at your leisure. Simply select a template from the Template Chooser to use it:

- To open the Template Chooser in OS X, press N or select File > New. Browse the templates, then click Choose in the lower right to open one.
- iOS Tap the Create Document icon in the Documents manager to open the Template Chooser. Browse the templates, select one, and tap to open it.
- Apple iCloud Click the Create Document icon in the Documents manager to open the Template Chooser. Browse the templates, choose one to use, and then click Choose to open it.

Text, images, or both are already present in templates. These texts and images serve as placeholders for the content you intend to include. Simply select the text box you want to work in and begin typing your text. The same method applies to graphics and images within the template; choose the one you want to replace and replace it with one of your own.

MAKING YOUR TEMPLATES

Apple, believe it or not, cannot always think of everything a user might require, so said user may have to supply something for herself from time to time. Consider templates: chances are you'll come up with a task for which you'll require a design template. If that's the case, it's simple enough to make your template. Keep in mind that this will necessitate using Pages for OS X; this feature is not supported by iOS or iCloud. To make your template in Pages for Mac, follow these steps:

1. Make a document with all the features you want in your template (you'll learn how to do this as we go through the book).
2. Select File > Save As Template from the menu.
3. Carry out one of the following actions:

- To make a template file to share with others or use on iOS devices, click the Save button, name the template, choose a location on your computer to save it to, or choose iCloud to make it available on all of your iOS devices, and click Save.

- Click the Add To Template Chooser button to instantly add your new template to the Pages for OS X Template Chooser. The template will now be visible in the Template Chooser, where you can give it a name.

ADDING CUSTOM PAGES TEMPLATES FOR OS X AND IOS

Custom templates are easy to add and remove from Pages for OS X and Pages for iOS.

To add a custom Pages template on macOS:

1. Create a new Pages document with the formatting, layout, and content that you want to use as a template.
2. Click on File > Save as Template from the top menu.
3. Choose a name for your template and select the category in which you want to save it. You can choose from Built-in or My Templates.
4. Click Save to add the new template to Pages.

To add a custom Pages template on iOS:

1. Create a new Pages document with the formatting, layout, and content that you want to use as a template.
2. Tap the ellipsis (three dots) button in the top right corner of the document.
3. Tap "Use as Template" from the menu.
4. Choose a name for your template and select the category in which you want to save it. You can choose from Built-in or My Templates.
5. Tap "Save" to add the new template to Pages.

Once you've added your custom template to Pages, you can use it to create new documents in the future. To do so:

1. Open Pages on your device.
2. Tap the + (plus) button to create a new document.
3. Select the category where you saved your custom template.
4. Tap on the template to use it as the basis for your new document.
5. Edit and customize the new document as needed and save it to your device.

Custom templates can save you time and effort by allowing you to create new documents quickly and easily using your preferred formatting and layout.

MAKING USE OF THIRD-PARTY PAGE TEMPLATES

To use third-party templates in Pages, you can start by doing a web search for "Pages templates" or "free Pages templates." Several websites offer a variety of templates, ranging from basic to advanced, that can be downloaded to your computer's hard drive. However, it's important to exercise caution when downloading templates from these websites as they may contain viruses or malware. It's recommended to download templates only from reputable sources and to use antivirus software to protect your computer.

Once you've found a template that you like, you can download it to your computer and then sync it with your iPad using the iTunes File Sharing syncing process described in the "Basic Features" section of Pages. Once you've synced the template to your device, you can open it in Pages and begin editing it to suit your needs.

It's important to note that when working with third-party templates, it's a good idea to duplicate the template document before beginning to work on it. This way, you'll always have a blank version of the template to use if needed, and you won't risk losing your original template.

Here are steps on how to do it:

1. Search for third-party templates online, and download the ones you want to use.
2. Open Pages for Mac and create a new document.
3. In the template chooser window, select "My Templates."
4. Click "Add" at the bottom of the window, and choose the third-party template you want to use.
5. The third-party template will be added to your "My Templates" folder, and you can use it for future documents.

In addition to using third-party templates, Pages also allows you to create your own templates. Although Pages doesn't provide an option to save templates in the Create New Document screen, you can save a regular Pages document as a template by simply creating a document with the desired styles, formatting, and elements, and then saving it as a regular Pages document. This document can then be used as a template by opening it and making the necessary changes.

Furthermore, if you've created new styles that you would like to use in all your documents, you can save them as the new default style for all your documents by going to Format > Advanced > Create Master from Current Page.

CHAPTER 4: WORKING WITH TEXT IN PAGES

Here, you'll begin learning how to use Pages to create documents that you can use. By the way, (loudly) chanting the T-E-X-T cheer in the title of this section is an excellent way to get motivated for the tasks ahead, but be cautious, as your sudden burst of energy may be unsettling to some housemates and coworkers.

TEXT INSERTION

Text can be added to almost anything on a computer or mobile device, so let's just get this one done. Simply open a new document in Pages for Mac and begin typing—that's all there is to it. A new blank document greets you by default with a blinking cursor, practically begging you to tap a few keys. If you're working with a template or a pre-formatted document, simply locate the area where you want to insert your text and begin typing. While it's all very basic, one feature we shouldn't overlook is the ability to confine text to a text box rather than allowing it to run wild throughout the document.

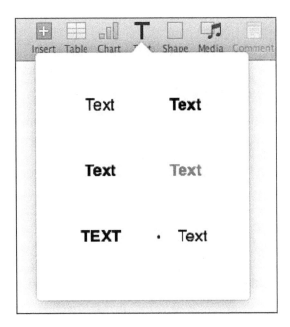

To make a text box, do the following:

1. In the toolbar, click the Text button; its icon is a T.
2. Select the type of text box you want to add and drag it from the Text window into your document.
3. To move the text box, simply click-and-hold the text and drag the box to the desired location. iOS Text can also be easily added to iOS documents. It doesn't get any easier if it's a new document. As in OS X, as soon as the new document opens, the cursor blinks at you, and you can begin typing as the on-screen keyboard also opens. If you misplace the keyboard, simply tap inside the document to reopen it and resume typing.

To add a text box to a document in Pages for iOS, follow these steps:

1. Tap the plus sign (+) in the upper right corner of the screen.
2. Tap the Text button, which, surprisingly, looks like a T.
3. Select the type of text you want in the text box, then tap-and-drag it into the document. You can tap and drag the text box any time to move it to a more convenient location. iCloud Adding text to iCloud for Pages is no more complicated than it is for other Pages versions. Again, the moment you open a new document, it is ready for you to enter text.

Adding a text box in iCloud is also very simple, with one minor difference:

1. Click the Text button in the toolbar at the top of the window; it looks like a T yet again.
2. Unlike in OS X or iOS Pages, the text box simply appears in the document; you cannot drag and drop it into place. However, once the text box is in the document, you can drag it wherever you want.

FONT SELECTION AND FORMATTING

When it comes to bringing a document to life, fonts are just as important as images. Who wants to look at a page full of boring old Times New Roman (no offense intended for Times New Roman fans among the readership) when there are so many other lively options? Pages app is adept at selecting and formatting fonts to match the style of whatever document you have in mind. OS X The Format bar is your friend in Pages for OS X, which is especially noticeable when working with text. When you select text in the document, the Text Format bar, as shown in the illustration, appears on the right side of the document window.

To select a font for your document, select one from the Font pop-up menu in the Format bar. The list is WYSIWYG (what you see is what you get), so you can choose what you want on the fly. Change the font's appearance by changing its typeface, size, and color from the Format bar. There are also options to make the text bold, italic, or underlined.

The Format bar's Alignment section allows you to align text to the left, center, or right side of your document and justify text (which aligns it to both the left and right margins). Using the Spacing section, adjust the spacing between text lines.

For more options, click the arrow next to spacing. **iOS** The on-screen keyboard is a godsend for Pages users. It provides a toolbar with buttons to format your text as you type quickly.

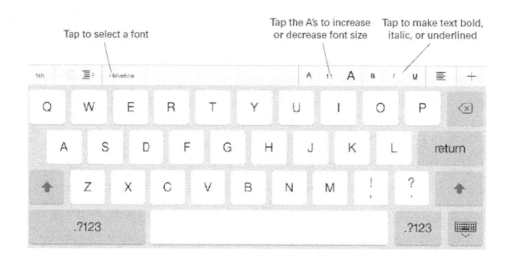

You can also use the format inspector to make changes to your text.

Changing the appearance of text in Pages for iCloud is nearly identical to changing the appearance of text in Pages for OS X. When you select text in the document, the format panel appears, which provides the same functionality as the Format bar in OS X Pages. However, font selection may be more limited.

Making Use of Paragraph Styles

At the click of a mouse, paragraph styles are pre-formatted sets of text attributes (such as a specific font, size, and color) that can be applied to sections of text or even entire documents (or tap of a finger). Each template employs paragraph styles for its various elements, and you can also apply them to new documents.

To use a paragraph style in Pages for OS X or iCloud, follow these steps:

1. Choose the text to which you want to apply the style.
2. Select Paragraph Styles from the Format bar of OS X or the Format panel of iCloud. 3. Scroll through the styles and choose the one you want to use, then click to apply it to the text.

To apply a paragraph style in iOS, follow these steps:

1. Choose the text to which you want to apply the style.
2. Select style from the format inspector icon.
3. Scroll through the styles to find the one you want to use, then tap to apply it to the text.

Making Lists

Lists, whether bulleted or numbered, are frequently used to assist readers in correctly understanding a subject by better organizing it for them. Pages is an expert at lists, as it is at almost everything else. Pages can do a lot of list formatting automatically by default, but you can always turn off automatic lists and manually change them. OS X Pages in OS X is a little more powerful than its siblings when it comes to listing creation and quite a bit more when it comes to iCloud.

To make a list in Pages for Mac:

1. Position the cursor where you want your list to start.
2. Begin by typing a bullet (OPTION-8), a number, or a letter (numbers and letters must be immediately followed by a period), and then type the first item in the list.
3. When you press the RETURN key, Pages switches to list mode.
4. Keep adding items to your list by typing them in and pressing RETURN after each one.
5. To stop the list from generating, press RETURN twice or the DELETE key.

You can quickly change the hierarchy of a list by dragging items in the list left or right or change the order by dragging an item up or down the list. When you start clicking and dragging an item, a blue arrow will appear to guide you to where it should go in your list.

To make a list in Pages for iOS, follow these steps:

1. Select the location in the document where you want your list to begin.
2. Begin typing a dash, a number, or a letter (numbers and letters must be immediately followed by a period), and then begin typing the first item in the list.
3. Press RETURN, and Pages switch to list mode.
4. Continue adding items to your list by typing them in and pressing the RETURN key after each one. By tapping the indent buttons in the keyboard toolbar, you can change the hierarchy of an item in the list (next to the TAB key).
5. To stop the list from being generated, press RETURN twice. You can easily change the hierarchy of a list, as with Pages for OS X, by touching and dragging items in the list left or right or by touching and dragging an item up or down the list. When you begin to click-and-drag an item, a blue arrow and blue alignment guides appear to assist with item placement.

To make a list in Pages for iCloud, follow these steps:

1. Enter the first item on your list and press the RETURN key. Rep this step until you've listed all of your items.
2. Choose the text to include in your list.
3. Locate the Bullets & Lists menu near the bottom of the Text format pane. Select one of the styling options from the menu for your list.
4. Add more items to your list by typing them out and pressing RETURN after each one. Using the indent buttons at the bottom of the Text format pane, you can change the hierarchy of an item in the list.
5. To stop the list from generating, select None from the Bullets & List menu in the Text format pane.

Working with Unique Characters

Special characters mean font characters that most of us don't need to use regularly. To use special characters in your Pages for OS X documents:

1. Position the cursor in the document where you want to insert the special character.
2. Open the Special Characters window by selecting Edit > Special Characters.
3. From the bottom of the window, choose a category and click a character to insert it into your document.

TEXT FLOW MODIFICATION

When you type text into a Pages document, it automatically flows from one page or column to the next. However, forcing the text to flow differently than the default may sometimes be necessary. Pages for

OS X and iOS allow you to easily change how text flows through your documents, but this feature is not yet available in Pages for iCloud. There are several ways to alter the text flow in Pages for OS X:

- **Break in the line:** Begin a new line within the same paragraph. To insert a line break, press SHIFT-RETURN.
- **Page break**: This forces text in the following line to start at the top of the next page. Select Page Break from the Insert menu in the toolbar.
- **Insert or delete text columns**: Choose the text for which you want to add or remove columns, then click the Layout tab in the Text format bar. Using the pop-up menu, increase or decrease the number of columns, and then check the Equal Column Width check box if you want your columns to be uniform in size.
- **Column break**: Makes text start at the top of the next column. Select Column Break from the Insert menu in the toolbar.
- **Page breaks and pagination**: Click the More tab in the Text Format bar to see the four Paginations & Break options:
  - *Keep all lines on the same page.* Allows all lines of a paragraph to remain on the same page.
  - *Continue with the next paragraph.* Maintain a paragraph on the same page as the one after it.
  - *Begin a new paragraph on a new page.* A paragraph is moved to the top of the next page.
  - *Avoid widows and orphan lines.* Ensures that a paragraph's first or last line is not separated from the rest of the paragraph on the previous or next page.

Pages for iOS also has a nice selection of text flow options:

- **Break in the line**: Begin a new line within the same paragraph. Tap where you want the break to go, tap + in the keyboard's toolbar (on the right), and then Line Break.
- **Page turn**: text in the next line is forced to begin at the top of the next page. Tap the break location in the document, tap the + icon in the keyboard's toolbar, followed by Page Break.
- **Insert or delete text columns**: Choose the text for which you want to add or remove columns, then tap the format inspector icon (paintbrush), followed by layout. Tap the + or - icons to increase or decrease the number of columns.
- **Break in the column**: Text is forced to begin at the top of the next column. Tap where you want the current column to end, then tap + on the keyboard's toolbar, followed by Column Break.

MAKING USE OF PHONETIC GUIDE TEXTS

Phonetic guide texts are useful in language learning and for clarifying pronunciation in written material. Mac and iOS devices support international keyboards, allowing you to enter text in various languages. Using any of the Japanese, Chinese, or Korean keyboards allows Pages to add features to the text that will help you or the reader better understand it. One of these features is phonetic guides, which help you pronounce the text more easily.

To create a phonetic guide text in Pages for Mac, follow these steps:

1. Select the text you want to add a phonetic guide to.
2. In the menu bar, click "Format" and then "Font."
3. In the "Font" window, check the box next to "Show" under "Character Viewer."
4. Open the Character Viewer by clicking the icon that appears in the menu bar, or by pressing "Control-Command-Space."
5. In the Character Viewer, select "Latin" from the left-hand column, then scroll down to "IPA Extensions" and select it.
6. Select the IPA symbol you want to use, and click "Insert."
7. Type the corresponding phonetic text after the symbol.
8. Continue adding symbols and corresponding text as needed.
9. Click "OK" to close the "Font" window.

To insert phonetic guide text in Pages for Mac, follow these steps:

1. Place the text cursor where you want to add the phonetic guide text.
2. In the top menu, select "Format" and then "Advanced".
3. Choose "Phonetic Guide" from the Advanced menu.
4. In the Phonetic Guide dialog box, enter the text for the pronunciation guide in the "Pronunciation" field.
5. Select the reading direction for the guide text, either horizontal or vertical.
6. Choose the font and font size for the phonetic guide text.
7. Click the "OK" button to add the phonetic guide text to your document.

To insert phonetic guide text in Pages for iOS, follow these steps:

1. Tap to place the text cursor where you want to add the phonetic guide text.
2. Tap the "Aa" button on the top menu to bring up the text formatting options.
3. Swipe left in the text formatting options until you see the "Phonetic Guide" option.
4. Tap "Phonetic Guide" to bring up the Phonetic Guide dialog box.
5. In the Pronunciation field, enter the text for the pronunciation guide.
6. Choose the reading direction for the guide text, either horizontal or vertical.

7. Select the font and font size for the phonetic guide text.

8. Tap "Done" to add the phonetic guide text to your document.

MAKING USE OF BIDIRECTIONAL TEXT

Some languages, like English, write from left to right on the page, whereas others, like Hebrew and Arabic, write from right to left. Pages for OS X and iOS (but not iCloud) include support for text in both directions or bidirectional text. Apple has gone global, you guys!

To use bidirectional text in Pages for OS X, follow these steps:

1. Select the text you want to change the direction of, or click to position the cursor on the line where you want to begin changing the text direction.

2. Select a language from the Input Source menu in the Finder's menu bar (upper right of your computer screen).

3. In the Text Format bar's Alignment section, click the text direction button (looks like two arrows facing in opposite directions). Quit and restart Pages if you don't see the button in the Alignment section.

4. Enter your text. The text will continue to enter the document in the direction specified by the text direction button.

5. To change the direction of the text, simply click the text direction button. Make sure to select the correct language from the Input Source menu.

To use bidirectional text in Pages for iOS, follow these steps:

1. Choose the text you want to change the direction of, or tap to place the cursor on the line where you want to begin changing the text direction.

2. Tap the globe button on the keyboard to select the language you want to use.

3. Select style from the format inspector icon.

4. Click the text direction button, which is located to the right of the alignment buttons (looks like two arrows pointing in opposite directions).

5. Enter your text. The text will continue to enter the document in the direction selected by the text direction button.

6. To change the direction, simply tap the text direction button again. Make sure you select the correct language by tapping the globe icon on the keyboard again.

CHOOSING A PAPER SIZE AND MARGINS

Pages for OS X and iOS allow you to change the paper size and margins for documents, but not Pages for iCloud (letter size is the only option as of this writing when creating a new document within Pages for iCloud). OS X Pages for OS X supports a wide range of standard paper sizes and uses paper sizes supported by your installed printers. Setting paper sizes and margins is a breeze with the Setup bar:

1. Begin by opening a document.
2. On the far right of the toolbar, click the Setup icon (a gear) and then the Document tab.
3. Carry out one or more of the following actions:
   - Change the paper size by selecting a printer from the size pop-up menu (Any Printer is the default) and selecting a supported size from the size pop-up menu.
   - Alter the page's orientation by selecting the portrait or landscape icon.
   - Change the values in the Document Margins section to adjust the margins.

In both Pages for OS X and iCloud, adding a header or footer is handled in the same way:

1. Hover your mouse pointer over the top or bottom areas of the page to see the header or footer blocks; there will be three blocks in both.
2. Edit the header or footer by clicking on either block; you can use as many blocks as you want.
3. Carry out one or more of the following actions:
   - Insert and format text in the header and footer blocks in the same way you would any other text.
   - In Pages for OS X, click the Insert Page Number button to add page numbers to a header or footer block.
   - In Pages for OS X, click the Insert icon in the toolbar and choose Page Count or Date & Time to add to a header or footer block.
   - In Pages for iCloud, click the Insert icon in the toolbar and select Page Number or Page Count to add either to a header or footer block.

Adding headers and footers in Pages for iOS is a little different but no less straightforward:

1. In the toolbar, tap the Tools icon, then Document Setup.
2. Tap the header or footer section to reveal its blocks and activate the keyboard.

SECTIONAL ORGANIZATION

Sectional organization in Pages allows you to divide your document into distinct sections that can have different formatting, headers, and footers. You can create sections in Pages for OS X, iOS, and iCloud using the following steps:

In Pages for OS X:

1. Place your cursor where you want to start the new section.
2. Click the "Insert" button on the top menu bar and choose "Section Break" from the drop-down menu.
3. A new section with a different set of formatting options will be added to your document. You can change the formatting of the new section by selecting it and making changes in the Format panel.

In Pages for iOS:

1. Place your cursor where you want to start the new section.
2. Tap the "Insert" button in the top toolbar, and choose "Section Break" from the list of options.
3. A new section with a different set of formatting options will be added to your document. You can change the formatting of the new section by selecting it and making changes in the formatting options.

In Pages for iCloud:

1. Place your cursor where you want to start the new section.
2. Click the "Insert" button on the top menu bar and choose "Section Break" from the drop-down menu.
3. A new section with a different set of formatting options will be added to your document. You can change the formatting of the new section by selecting it and making changes in the formatting options.

Once you've created a section break, you can format the new section independently from the rest of the document. For example, you can apply a different header or footer to the new section or change the margins, orientation, and page numbering. You can also change the layout and formatting of the text within the new section without affecting the rest of the document.

Pages for OS X allows you to add background colors and borders to pages or paragraphs in your document, but the iOS and iCloud versions do not (as of this moment). To add a background color, do the following:

- Choose the paragraph to which you want to add the background color, or press A to select the entire page and apply the color to it.
- In the Text pane, click the Layout tab and then the Format inspector icon.
- Select Borders & Rules by clicking the arrow next to it.

- To see a list of available colors, click the box next to Background Color, and then click one to apply it. If you're feeling particularly sporty, you can use the color wheel to create your own color.

To include a border:

1. Choose the paragraph to which you want to apply the border, or use A to select the entire page and apply the border to it.
2. In the Text pane, click the Layout tab and then the Format inspector icon.
3. Select Borders & Rules by clicking the arrow next to it.
4. From the available options, choose a line type, color, and line thickness. You can also change the border's position and offset.

EXAMINING FORMATTING MARKS

Formatting marks, also known as invisible, are nonprinting marks that appear on the page when you press RETURN or TAB or insert elements like line breaks and page breaks. They are useful to see at times, such as when viewing your page layout, so we need a way to see them. Pages in OS X has a direct way to see these marks, Pages in iOS has a more indirect way, and Pages for iCloud hasn't evolved that capability yet.

To show and hide formatting marks in Pages for Mac, you can follow these steps:

1. Click on the "View" menu in the top menu bar.
2. Select "Show Invisibles" to display the formatting marks, or "Hide Invisibles" to hide them.

To show and hide formatting marks in Pages for iOS, you can follow these steps:

1. Tap the three-dot icon in the top right corner of the screen to access the Settings menu.
2. Tap "Document Setup" to open the Document Setup screen.
3. Tap the toggle switch next to "Show Invisibles" to turn the display of formatting marks on or off.

USING ENDNOTES AND FOOTNOTES

Endnotes are notes at the end of a document, whereas footnotes appear at the bottom of a page. Pages for OS X and iOS allow you to add footnotes and endnotes to documents, but Pages for iCloud only will enable you to add footnotes.

When you add a note to Pages in OS X, it is initially treated as a footnote, but you can easily convert it to an endnote later (and all other notes will change as well).

To add a footnote in Pages for Mac:

1. Place your cursor where you want to insert the footnote.
2. From the menu bar, select Insert > Footnote. Alternatively, you can press Command + Option + F.

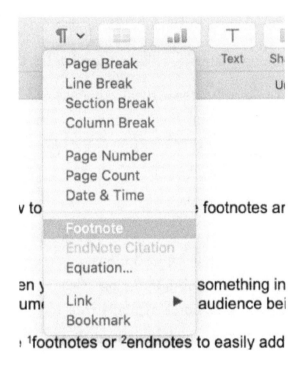

3. A superscript number will appear at the insertion point and the footnote text will appear at the bottom of the page. Type the text you want to appear in the footnote.

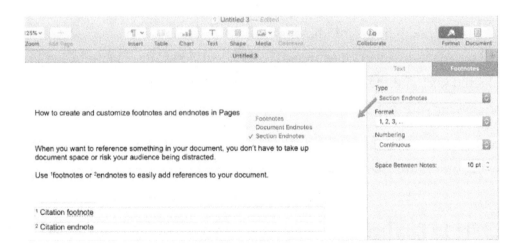

To change a footnote to an endnote (or vice versa):

1. Click any note on the page; all notes are selected, as indicated by the blue boxes surrounding them.
2. In the toolbar, click the Format button.
3. Change the type, format, and numbering of your notes using the options in the Footnotes tab of the Format bar. Remove a note quickly by moving your cursor to the right of the note's symbol in the document text and pressing the DELETE key. All other notes will be reorganized automatically to reflect the change. By default, iOS Pages treats your first note as a footnote.

You can easily convert it to an endnote later, just like in Pages for OS X. To add a footnote:

1. Tap the text to which the note will refer in the document.
2. In the keyboard's toolbar, tap + and then Footnote. The note symbol appears next to the selected text, and the cursor moves to the bottom of the page.
3. Fill in the text for your note.

To change a footnote to an endnote (or vice versa):

1. Tap any note on the page; every note is selected, as indicated by the blue boxes surrounding it.
2. Select the Format inspector icon, then select Options.
3. Make changes to the type, format, and numbering of your notes. To quickly remove a note, move your cursor to the right of the note's symbol in the document text and press the DELETE key. All other notes will be reorganized automatically to reflect the change.

Pages for iCloud provides only one type of note you can create: footnotes. It will, however, retain endnotes added to documents using the OS X or iOS versions, so don't worry about reformatting your footnotes to endnotes. To add a footnote:

1. Select the text to which the note will refer in the document. Be careful with cursor placement, or the note may end up in the middle of a word.
2. In the toolbar, click the Insert button and then select Footnote. The note symbol appears next to the selected text, and the cursor moves to the bottom of the page.
3. Fill in the text for your note.

To delete a note, move your cursor to the right of the note's symbol in the document text and press the DELETE key. All other notes will be reorganized automatically to reflect the change.

CREATING A TABLE OF CONTENTS

When it comes to quickly finding a topic in a document, tables of contents are the bomb. Pages for OS X makes it surprisingly simple to include a table of contents for an entire document or a section(s). Pages for iOS and iCloud do not support adding tables of contents, but they will be retained when editing a document in one of them. To include a table of contents in a document or section, do the following:

1. Position the cursor in the document where you want the table of contents to be inserted.
2. Select Insert > Table Of Contents from the menu (rather than the Insert button in the toolbar) and one of the following options:
   - Document Generates a table of contents for the entire document
   - Section Generates a table of contents for the section in which the cursor is located; Creates a table of contents for contents found between this table of contents and the next table of contents.
4. Once your table of contents has appeared, click the Format button in the toolbar to bring up the Table of Contents pane. Check the box to the left of each document element that Pages should use to populate your table of contents. Check the box in the #'s column if you want the page numbers of the elements to appear in the table of contents.

CHAPTER 5: ENHANCING YOUR DOCUMENTS WITH PAGES

Now that you've mastered the fundamentals of creating a word processing document in Pages, it's time to add some flair to the proceedings. With pages, you can insert images and graphics into your documents, use audio and video to enhance your Pages files, use tables to your advantage, and place and edit your charts.

Let me be clear: there's nothing wrong with a document that's only text, even if it's in a simple font like Courier, as long as the content is worthwhile. Everyone knows that images, shapes, and multimedia are required to spice up an otherwise excellent document!

Graphics and media aren't just there to take up space (usually); they're also there to provide information on their own. Using colors in a document can help convey the text's tone. By clearly displaying the document's object, images can save you a thousand words (for example, interior and exterior pictures of a home in a sales flyer). Multimedia, such as audio and video, can go even further by adding a visual and auditory dimension in addition to text and pictures.

Tables and charts also aid in the communication of information in a document. They both take otherwise complex and overwhelming information and deconstruct it into (hopefully) well-organized and manageable bite-sized morsels. A long and tedious list can be much easier to digest in table form, and a slew of numbers can be much more useful to a reader when represented graphically. Pages is fantastic at adding all of these items to your documents, and it does so in its typical simple manner without sacrificing effectiveness.

Pages refers to "objects" as anything that can be placed on a document. Images, graphics, and shapes are all examples of "objects" (text boxes do, too, technically speaking). Pages makes it simple to insert objects into your documents. Working with them once they're in place is a pleasure rather than a chore, thanks to Apple's team of iWork developers' focus on usability and functionality. Pages refers to multimedia, which includes audio and video, as "media." Anyone who has listened to iTunes or watched YouTube can affirm that media offers another avenue for communicating your message to its intended audience. In this section, I'll show you how to incorporate objects and media into your documents and manipulate and enhance their impact.

ADDING IMAGES TO DOCUMENTS

An image is powerful, and no other form of media conveys a message and packs an emotional punch quite like images, whether it's a photo of a waterfall, a sunset, or a flower, or perhaps an unforgettable snapshot of your grandparents captured in the joy of an intimately sweet moment. I'll make a wild guess and say that no other computer manufacturer realizes this concept better than Apple. It has ensured that iWork users can use images in simple and powerful ways. Let's look at how Pages can assist you in inserting images into your documents.

Getting images into a document is the first step in working with them, but it is the most important. Remember that many of the templates included with Pages already include images, but these are placeholders that should be replaced with your images.

To insert an image in Pages for Mac:

1. Click on the location in your document where you want to insert the image.
2. Drag an image from the Finder or a folder and drop it onto the document. You can also copy an image and paste it directly into the document.
3. Alternatively, you can click on the "Insert" menu in the menu bar and select "Choose" to browse for an image on your Mac and insert it into the document.

To insert an image in Pages for iOS:

1. Tap on the "+" button on the toolbar or tap on an image placeholder.

2. Select an image from your device's photo library or Files app, or take a new photo using the camera.

3. The image will be inserted into the document at the location of the cursor.

To replace an image in Pages for Mac or iOS:

1. Click on the image you want to replace to select it.

2. Drag a new image from the Finder or a folder and drop it onto the selected image. The new image will replace the old one.

3. Alternatively, you can right-click on the selected image and choose "Replace Image" to browse for a new image on your Mac or device.

To remove an image in Pages for Mac or iOS:

1. Click on the image you want to remove to select it.

2. Press the delete key on your keyboard or right-click on the selected image and choose "Delete." The image will be removed from the document.

IMAGE MASKING

Image masking is a technique used in graphic design and image editing to selectively hide or reveal parts of an image. With image masking, you can create complex effects that blend two or more images together seamlessly, or isolate an object in an image to make it easier to work with.

In Pages version 12.2.1, you can use the Instant Alpha tool to perform basic image masking on an image. Here's how to use the Instant Alpha tool:

1. Open Pages on your Mac device.

2. Open the document that contains the image you want to mask.

3. Click on the image to select it.

4. Click on the "Format" menu in the menu bar and select "Image."

5. In the Image panel, click on the "Instant Alpha" button. The cursor will change to a pointer with a magic wand icon.

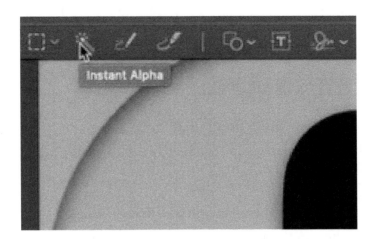

6. Click and drag the cursor over the parts of the image you want to mask. The areas you select will be highlighted in purple.

7. If you accidentally select an area you don't want to mask, click on it to deselect it.

8. When you're done selecting the areas you want to mask, press the delete key on your keyboard to remove the selected areas. The deleted areas will be replaced with a transparent background.

9. You can adjust the sensitivity of the Instant Alpha tool by using the slider at the bottom of the Image panel. Moving the slider to the right will make the tool more sensitive, while moving it to the left will make it less sensitive.

REMOVING IMAGE ELEMENTS

You may decide to remove a background color from an image or only want one element of an image to appear in your document, such as a person but not the environment around them. Both can be accomplished using the Instant Alpha tool in Pages for OS X and iOS (sorry, iCloud users, but this isn't supported).

To use Instant Alpha in Pages for OS X, follow these steps:

1. Click on the image you want to edit to select it.

2. Click on the "Format" menu in the menu bar and select "Image."

3. In the Image panel, click on the "Instant Alpha" button.

4. Use the targeting tool to select the area of the image you want to remove. The area will be highlighted in purple.

5. Click and drag over the area to remove it. Hold down the Option key to remove all instances of the selected color or element at once.

6. If you remove an area you didn't intend to, hold down the Shift key and drag over it to restore it.

7. When you're done removing the unwanted elements, click "Done" to save your changes.

CHANGING THE COLOR LEVELS IN AN IMAGE

Pages for OS X includes an image feature that the other two versions of Pages do not: the ability to adjust color levels in an image. To make color changes to an image in Pages for Mac:

1. Click on the image you want to edit to select it.
2. Click on the "Format" menu in the menu bar and select "Image."
3. In the Image panel, click on the "Adjust Image" button.
4. Use the sliders and controls in the Adjust Image panel to adjust the color levels of the image. You can adjust the exposure, contrast, highlights, shadows, saturation, and more.
5. As you adjust the sliders, the image will update in real-time so you can see the effect of your changes.
6. If you want to restore the original color settings, click on the "Restore" button at the bottom of the Adjust Image panel.
7. When you're done making adjustments, click "Done" to save your changes.

ADDING TABLES TO YOUR DOCUMENTS

Before learning to work within a table, you must get one into a document. Pages is a champ at this little feat, regardless of version. OS X To add a table to a document in Pages for OS X:

1. Place the cursor where you'd like the table to appear in the document.
2. Click the Table icon in the toolbar.
3. Click to choose a table from the options, or drag one from the menu and drop it into the document. Use the left and right arrows in the menu to see different types.
4. Click a cell and begin typing to add content to it.
5. To move a table, click to activate it, then click and drag the circle in its upper left corner.
6. Delete a table by clicking the circle in its upper left corner and pressing the DELETE key.

To add a table to a document in Pages for iOS:

1. Tap to place the cursor where you want the table to appear in the document.
2. Tap + in the toolbar, then the Table icon, to see a list of available tables.
3. Tap to select a table from the options, or drag one from the menu and drop it into the document. Swipe to the left or right to see more options.
4. Tap a cell and begin typing to add content to it.

5. To move a table, tap it to activate it, tap-and-drag the circle in its upper left corner.

6. Delete a table by tapping it and then tapping Delete in the menu.

To add a table to a document in Pages for iCloud:

1. Place the cursor where you'd like the table to reside in the document.

2. Click the Table icon in the toolbar.

3. Click to choose a table from the options.

4. To add content to a cell, click it and start typing.

5. To move a table, activate it by clicking on it, then drag the square in its upper left corner.

6. Select a table by clicking its upper left corner and then pressing the DELETE key to delete a table.

ADDING A SHAPE

Click the shape button or select Insert > Shape from the top menu to insert a shape into a document.

This will bring up all the shapes available for you. Find the one you like and click it to insert it.

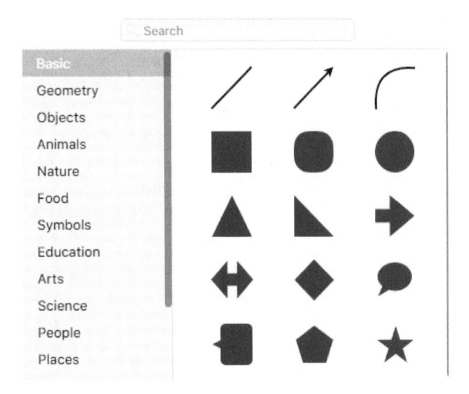

Remember that you can later change the color, border, and shadow/reflection effects! Shapes sound a little deceptive. If you're anything like me, you're probably thinking square, circle, etc. However, shapes in Pages are similar to clipart. Yes, there are basic shapes, but there are also other things.

To add a shape to Pages for iOS, follow these steps:

1. Tap the + icon in the upper right corner.
2. Tap the Shape button (it looks like a square) to see the available shapes. To see more shapes in the menu, swipe left or right.
3. Drag a shape into your document by tapping it.
4. Drag the shape to the desired location in your document.
5. Drag the handles to change the shape's size.

To add a shape to Pages for iCloud, follow these steps:

1. In the toolbar, click the Shape button. Unlike Pages for OS X and iOS, there is only one screen, so don't try to see more; you'll just wear out your mouse button.
2. Drag the shape into position by clicking and dragging it.
3. Change the color and other attributes of the shape using the options in the Shape tab of the format panel.

ADDING A CHART

Here are the steps for adding a chart to your Pages document:

1. Tap where you want the chart to appear in your document.
2. Tap the "Insert" button in the toolbar.
3. Tap on "Charts" in the Insert menu.
4. Choose the chart type (bar, area, line, or pie) and style you want to use.
5. Select a color scheme from the options available (2D, 3D, or interactive).
6. Tap on your preferred chart to insert it into your document.
7. Alternatively, you can also add a chart using the top menu by selecting "Insert" and then "Chart".

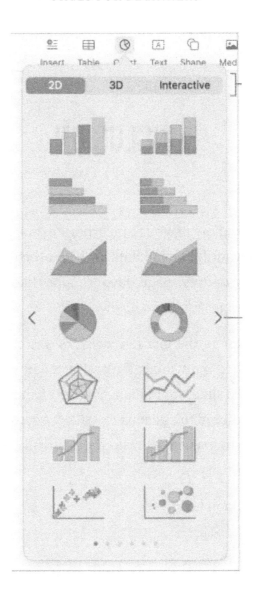

Once you've chosen your chart and inserted it into your document, you can then modify it by tapping on the chart to reveal the Chart Inspector. From there, you can edit the chart type, style, data, and more.

CONCLUSION

Pages is capable of page layout, allowing you to incorporate images and graphics and use fonts and colors creatively to create beautiful documents such as brochures and fliers. While Pages isn't meant to replace true heavy-duty page layout apps like Adobe's InDesign or Quark's QuarkXPress, it can produce stunning results on its own.

Almost everyone using a computer in the last few decades has created a document using a word processing program. Many of those individuals have also toiled over copious amounts of data in spreadsheet applications or created slides for audiences large or small in presentation software. Many different applications have been offered to assist users with these three tasks—some very well, some not so well—but all have seemed to make each task more difficult than it needed to be. Thus, Apple comes to the rescue!

Thank you for reading this book. Good luck.

NUMBERS
FOR BEGINNERS

The Most Updated Crash Course to Numbers |
Learn All the Functions, Macros, and Formulas
to Become a Pro in 7 Days or Less

ANDREW BLAKE

CHAPTER 1: INTRODUCTION

The Numbers app is a powerful spreadsheet application that lets you create, edit, and share spreadsheets on your iPhone or iPad. With Numbers, you can easily create beautiful charts and graphs, perform complex calculations, and easily share your work with others.

Numbers are the perfect tool for students, professionals, and anyone who needs to track and analyze data. Numbers is the perfect app for the job, whether you're tracking your expenses, keeping track of your fitness goals, or monitoring your investment portfolio.

With its intuitive interface and powerful features, Numbers is the perfect spreadsheet application for Mac, iPhone and iPad users.

The Numbers app for Apple products is a powerful tool that makes it easy to create beautiful spreadsheets. Here are some of its notable features:

A USER-FRIENDLY INTERFACE

One of the most notable features of the Numbers app is its user-friendly interface. The app is designed with a clean and simple layout, with menus and buttons that are easy to understand and navigate. This makes it easy for users, even those who have never used the app before, to create and edit spreadsheets quickly and efficiently.

The interface of the Numbers app is organized into several sections, including the main menu, the toolbar, and the sidebar. The main menu provides access to all the main features of the app, such as formatting, chart creation, and formula creation. The toolbar provides quick access to commonly used tools, such as font and cell formatting, and the sidebar provides access to additional features, such as tables and media.

The app also has a consistent design across all of its features, which makes it easy for users to learn and use new features quickly. The various menus and options are easy to understand and are labeled clearly, so users can easily find the features they need.

Another aspect of the user-friendly interface is the ability to customize the layout to suit individual preferences. Users can customize the toolbar to include only the tools they need, which makes the app more efficient to use. Additionally, users can customize the appearance of the app, including the background color and font style.

AN ARRAY OF CUSTOMIZABLE TEMPLATES

The templates provided by Numbers are fully customizable, allowing users to edit the design and structure of the template to suit their specific needs. Users can change the font, color scheme, and layout of the template, as well as add or remove tables, charts, and other data structures.

In addition to pre-designed templates, Numbers also provides users with the ability to create custom templates. Users can create a custom template by selecting a blank spreadsheet and adding their own tables, charts, and other data structures. This feature is useful for users who have specific needs that are not met by the pre-designed templates.

One of the most significant advantages of the template feature in Numbers is that it saves time and effort. Users can select a pre-designed template and customize it to suit their needs, without having to spend hours designing the spreadsheet from scratch. This feature is especially useful for users who need to create a spreadsheet quickly or who are not experienced in spreadsheet design.

Another benefit of the template feature is that it ensures consistency in design and structure. By using a pre-designed template, users can ensure that their spreadsheet follows a consistent layout and design, which makes it easier to read and understand.

CUSTOMIZABLE CELLS

Another notable feature of the Numbers app is its ability to customize individual cells within a spreadsheet. One of the most useful cell customization features in Numbers is the ability to format text. Users can adjust the font style, size, and color of text within individual cells or groups of cells. They can also format numbers to display as currency, percentage, or decimal, depending on their preference.

Numbers also allows users to adjust the borders around individual cells or groups of cells. Users can adjust the thickness and color of the borders, as well as add or remove individual borders. This feature is useful for creating tables or grids within a spreadsheet and making them more visually appealing.

Another powerful cell customization feature in Numbers is the ability to apply conditional formatting to specific cells. This feature allows users to set specific formatting rules based on the values within the cell. For example, users can set a rule to highlight any cell that contains a certain value or a value that falls within a specific range.

In addition to formatting text, borders, and applying conditional formatting, Numbers also allows users to add or delete rows and columns within a spreadsheet. This feature is useful for adjusting the layout of a spreadsheet or for adding new data to an existing spreadsheet.

ADVANCED FORMULAS AND FUNCTIONS

The Numbers app provides advanced formulas and functions that allow users to perform complex calculations quickly and easily. These formulas and functions are designed to help users save time and increase accuracy in their spreadsheets, making the app an essential tool for professionals who need to perform calculations regularly.

One of the most useful advanced formulas in Numbers is the SUMIF function. This function allows users to sum a range of cells that meet specific criteria. For example, users can use this function to sum all the sales that were made in a specific month or by a specific salesperson.

Another powerful formula in Numbers is the VLOOKUP function. This function allows users to find and retrieve data from a specific range of cells based on a specific value. For example, users can use this function to retrieve a customer's contact information based on their name or customer ID.

The Numbers app also includes a range of statistical functions, such as AVERAGE, STDEV, and COUNT. These functions are designed to help users analyze data and make informed decisions based on their findings.

In addition to the built-in formulas and functions, Numbers also allows users to create their own custom formulas. This feature is beneficial for users who need to perform calculations that are not included in the app's built-in formulas.

CHARTS AND GRAPHS

As you create spreadsheets in the Numbers app, you may want to use charts and graphs to visualize your data. Charts and graphs can assist in making your data easier to comprehend and interpret.

Numerous charts and graphs are available in Numbers, so selecting the right one for your data is critical. In general, you should use a graph or chart when you have numerical data that you want to visualize.

Some common reasons to use charts and graphs in Numbers include:

- To compare two or more sets of data
- To spot trends in your data
- To see relationships between different variables
- To make your data more understandable

When choosing a chart or graph, you must consider the type of data you have and what you want to accomplish with it. For example, if you have data that changes over time, you may want to use a line graph. A bar chart may be better if you want to compare different data sets.

Once you've selected the right chart or graph, you can use the built-in tools in Numbers to customize it to your liking.

If you're unsure which chart or graph to use, try experimenting with different options until you find one that works best for your data.

Charts and graphs are a great way to see patterns and trends in your data and can be helpful in understanding complex information. The Numbers app offers various charts and graphs, including line graphs, bar graphs, pie charts, and scatter plots.

You can create a wide range of charts and graphs in the Numbers app on your Apple device. Here are a few of the most well-known:

- **Bar Chart**: A bar chart is similar to a column chart, but the bars are horizontal instead of vertical. It is often used to compare data across different categories.
- **Pie Chart**: A pie chart is used to show how different components contribute to a whole. It is often used to display the percentage of revenue that comes from different product lines or the proportion of the budget that is allocated to different departments.
- **Line Graph**: Is used to show trends in data over time. It is often used to display stock prices, weather patterns, and other data that changes over time.
- **Area Graph**: Is used to show changes in data over time, but the area under the line is shaded to emphasize the cumulative values. It is often used to display sales figures or website traffic over time.
- **Scatter Plot**: Is used to show the relationship between two variables. It is often used to display data from scientific experiments, such as the relationship between temperature and pressure.

As you can see, the Numbers app provides users with a wide range of well-known charts and graphs that can be used to visualize data effectively. By choosing the right chart or graph for their data and customizing its appearance, users can communicate their findings effectively and make informed decisions based on their data. Experiment with different types to see which is best for your data set.

COMPATIBILITY WITH OTHER APPLE PRODUCTS

The Numbers app is designed to be fully compatible with other Apple products, including Mac computers, iPhones, and iPads. This means that users can seamlessly move between different Apple devices and continue working on their spreadsheets without interruption.

For example, a user can start working on a Numbers spreadsheet on their Mac computer, save it to iCloud, and then continue working on it on their iPhone or iPad. Any changes made on one device will be automatically synced to the other devices, ensuring that the user always has the most up-to-date version of their spreadsheet.

In addition to seamless syncing between devices, Numbers is also fully compatible with other Apple apps, such as Pages and Keynote. This means that users can easily import data from Numbers into Pages or Keynote to create reports, presentations, and other documents.

Another way that Numbers is compatible with other Apple products is through its support for Apple Pencil. Users can use an Apple Pencil to draw and write directly on their spreadsheets, which is particularly useful for adding annotations, highlighting important data points, or making calculations by hand.

The Numbers app has features to help you get the most out of your data. Here's a quick rundown of some of the things you can do:

- View and edit your data in a spreadsheet-like interface
- Apply formulas to perform calculations on your data
- Create charts and graphs for a better presentation of your statistics
- Share your data with others via email or social media
- Save your data as a CSV file to use in other apps.

CHAPTER 2: CREATING AND CUSTOMIZING FORMS IN NUMBERS

You might want to create a custom form in Numbers for many reasons. Perhaps you need a specific format for data entry or want to create a survey that can be easily shared and completed online. For this reason, creating a custom form in Numbers is easy.

Creating a custom form in Numbers starts with choosing the type of form you want to create. There are three main forms: data entry, questionnaires, and surveys.

Data entry forms are designed for easy data entry. They typically have a simple layout with fields for each piece of information you want to collect.

Questionnaires are similar to data entry forms but include questions that help gather information about a specific topic.

Surveys are forms that are designed to be completed by a large number of people. They typically include questions about various topics and can be distributed online or in person.

Once you've chosen the type of form you want to create, you can start customizing it to fit your needs. For example, you can add or delete fields, change the order of fields, or add custom questions.

You can also customize the look of your form by changing the colors, fonts, and layout. And if you're creating a survey, you can add a logo or image to the form.

Creating a custom form in Numbers is a great way to collect data specific to your needs. And with a little bit of customization, you can create a form that's uniquely yours.

HOW TO CREATE A FORM IN NUMBERS

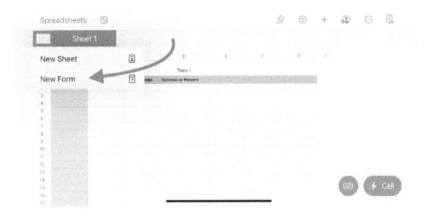

Creating a form in Numbers is a simple process that you can complete in just a few steps.

1. Open the Numbers app on your Mac.
2. Click on "New Document" to create a new spreadsheet.
3. From the template chooser, select the "Forms" category on the left-hand side.
4. Choose a form template that best fits your needs, or click "Blank" to create a custom form from scratch.
5. Start by customizing the form by adding fields, such as text boxes, checkboxes, radio buttons, or drop-down menus, using the "Add Field" button located in the top-right corner of the screen.
6. Use the "Inspector" panel to customize the form's appearance and behavior, such as the font, color, and formatting of the fields.
7. Once you have added all the fields you need, you can share your form by clicking the "Share" button in the top-right corner of the screen, selecting a sharing option, and sending the link to your recipients.

That's all there is to it! Creating a form in Numbers is quick and easy and can be a great way to collect information from people. Give it a try today.

HOW TO CUSTOMIZE A FORM IN NUMBERS

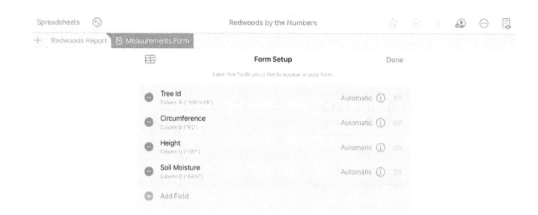

In Numbers, you can customize your forms to suit your needs better. To do this, follow these steps:

1. Open the Numbers app and create a new form by selecting the "Blank" template from the list of available templates.

2. Once the form is open, click on the "Fields" button in the top right corner of the screen. This will display a list of available fields that can be added to the form.

3. To add a field to the form, simply drag and drop it from the list of available fields onto the form. Users can add as many fields as they need to capture all of the information they require.

4. To customize the appearance of the form, users can use the formatting tools in the "Style" tab. This allows users to change the font, color, and other visual elements of the form to make it more visually appealing and easier to read.

5. To further customize the form, users can add images or other visual elements. To do this, select the "Media" button and then select the image or other media element that you want to add to the form.

6. Once the form is complete, users can share it with others by clicking on the "Share" button in the top right corner of the screen. This will allow users to send the form via email, message, or other means.

HOW TO USE CONDITIONAL FORMATTING IN FORM

Conditional formatting is a useful feature in Numbers that allows you to highlight important data in your forms automatically. This can help you to draw attention to specific data, making it easier to understand and analyze. Here's a guide on how to use conditional formatting in forms in Numbers:

1. Open the form that you want to add conditional formatting to in Numbers.
2. Select the cells that you want to apply conditional formatting to.
3. Click on the "Format" button in the top-right corner of the screen, then click on "Conditional Highlighting" from the dropdown menu.
4. Choose the type of conditional formatting that you want to apply. You can choose from a variety of options, including "Greater Than," "Less Than," "Between," and "Text Contains."
5. Set the formatting options for the selected cells. For example, if you choose the "Greater Than" option, you can set a threshold value and a color for cells that are greater than that value.
6. Click the "Apply" button to apply the conditional formatting to the selected cells.

HOW TO TEST A FORM

If you're a beginner and want to test forms in Numbers, here are some simple steps to follow:

- Preview the form: First, open the form you want to test and click on the "Preview" button located in the top-right corner of the screen. This will allow you to see what the form looks like to someone who will be filling it out.
- Test each field: Next, fill out each field to make sure it works correctly. Try entering different types of data, such as numbers, text, and dates, and see if the form accepts them. If any fields have validation rules, test those rules to make sure they work correctly.
- Submit the form: Once you have filled out the form, click on the "Submit" button to see if the form submits the data as expected. If the form is set up to send a confirmation email or message, check to make sure that you receive it.
- Review the data: After submitting the form, go to the "Responses" tab to see if the data was saved correctly. Check to make sure that all the data you entered is there and that it was saved in the correct format.
- Make adjustments: If you find any issues or errors during testing, make adjustments to the form as needed. You can make changes to the form layout, fields, and validation rules to improve the user experience.

Testing forms in Numbers is an essential step to ensure that the forms work as expected and that they provide a smooth user experience. By following these steps, you can test your forms in Numbers and make sure that they are functional, easy to use, and user-friendly.

HOW TO SHARE YOUR FORM IN NUMBERS

You can use the Share feature in Numbers when you want to share your form with others. It will allow you to share your form as a PDF or spreadsheet. To share your form:

1. Open the form that you want to share in Numbers.
2. Click on the "Share" button in the top-right corner of the screen. This will open the sharing options.
3. Select the method of sharing that you want to use. You can choose to share the form via email, message, or other means.
4. If you choose to share the form via email or message, enter the email or phone number of the recipient in the appropriate field. You can also add a message to the recipient.
5. Choose the format of the form that you want to share. You can choose to share the form in Numbers, Excel, or PDF format.
6. Click the "Share" button to send the form to the recipient.

Choose where you want to share your form. You can share it via email, Messages, Airdrop, or any other compatible app on your device.

TIPS FOR CREATING AND CUSTOMIZING FORMS IN NUMBER

Creating and customizing forms in Numbers can be an easy and straightforward process if you keep a few tips in mind. Here are some tips for creating and customizing forms in Numbers:

1. **Choose the right form template:** Numbers provides a variety of templates to choose from. Select the template that is best suited for your specific needs. This can help you save time and create forms that are both functional and visually appealing.
2. **Customize your form:** Customize the form to include fields and information that you require. This can help you capture all the necessary information in one place.
3. **Preview your form:** Before sharing your form with others, preview it to ensure that it looks the way you want it to. This can help you catch any errors or formatting issues before it is shared.
4. **Share your form:** Once your form is complete, you can share it with others. Numbers provides various options for sharing your form, such as sending it via email, message, or printing it.
5. **Use consistent formatting:** Consistency in formatting can help to make your form more professional and easier to read. Use the same font and font size throughout the form, and make sure that the fields are properly aligned.
6. **Keep it simple:** A simple form is often more effective than a complex one. Keep your form as simple as possible by only including the necessary fields and information.

7. **Use conditional formatting:** Use conditional formatting to highlight important information in your form. This can help to draw attention to specific fields, making it easier for users to quickly understand the information presented.

8. **Test the form:** Before sharing the form with others, test it to ensure that it is working as intended. This can help you to catch any errors or issues with the form before it is shared.

9. **Consider using automation:** Numbers provides a variety of automation options that can help to streamline the form creation process. Consider using automation to speed up data entry or to perform calculations automatically.

By following these additional tips, you can create forms in Numbers that are effective, efficient, and easy to use. By keeping the form simple, using consistent formatting, and testing the form before sharing it, you can ensure that the form meets your needs and is easy for others to use.

CHAPTER 3: ANALYZING DATA WITH PIVOT TABLES

WHAT IS A PIVOT TABLE?

A pivot table allows one to summarize and analyze data in Apple Numbers. You can use pivot tables to calculate summaries, find trends, and even spot outliers in your data. Pivot tables are simple to make and can be helpful to any Numbers spreadsheet.

You might want to use a pivot table in Apple Numbers for many reasons. Perhaps you have a large dataset to summarize, or you want to look for trends in your data. Pivot tables can be an invaluable tool for any Numbers user. Pivot tables are used for data analysis, allowing you to summarize and compare large amounts of data quickly. The Numbers app for Apple devices makes it easy to create and use pivot tables. A pivot table can be extremely useful when working with large amounts of data. They also allow you to quickly summarize and compare large amounts of data without wading through all the details.

CREATING PIVOT TABLES IN NUMBERS

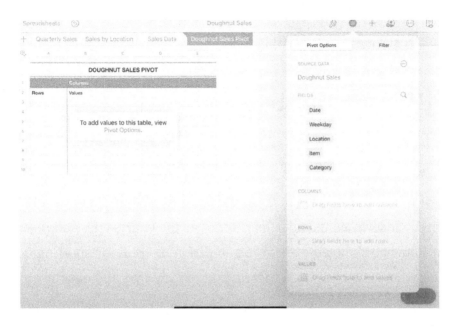

Pivot tables are a powerful tool for analyzing large data sets and identifying trends and patterns. In Numbers, creating pivot tables is a straightforward process that can be done in just a few steps. Here's how to create pivot tables in Numbers:

- Open your spreadsheet: First, open the Numbers spreadsheet that contains the data you want to analyze.

- Select your data: Next, select the data you want to include in your pivot table. Make sure that your data is organized in columns and rows, with each column containing a header.

- Create a new table: After selecting your data, go to the "Table" menu and select "New Table". This will create a new table in your spreadsheet.

- Add fields to your table: In the new table, you'll see a "Fields" pane on the right side of the screen. Drag the headers of the columns you want to include in your pivot table into the "Rows" or "Columns" area of the Fields pane. You can also drag headers into the "Values" area to summarize your data.

- Customize your table: Once you've added your fields, you can customize your pivot table by rearranging the headers, applying filters, and adding calculations.

- Refresh your table: If you make changes to the original data in your spreadsheet, you'll need to refresh your pivot table to see the changes. To do this, click on the "Refresh" button in the top-left corner of your pivot table.

By following these steps, you can create pivot tables in Numbers and use them to analyze and summarize your data. Pivot tables are a great way to get a high-level view of your data and identify trends and patterns that might be difficult to see otherwise. With Numbers, creating pivot tables is easy and can be done in just a few simple steps.

USING PIVOT TABLES TO IDENTIFY TRENDS

Now that we know how to make a pivot table, let's see how we can use it to find trends. There are several approaches to this, including using pivot charts, filters, and sorts.

One way to use pivot tables to find trends is to create a pivot chart. After creating your pivot table, choose "Chart" from the Insert menu, and select "Line" as the chart type. The resulting line chart will show you how your data has changed over time and can be helpful for spotting trends. For example, you might notice that your sales have been increasing steadily over the past few months.

Another approach is to use the filter feature. With your pivot table selected, go to the Data menu and select "Filter." In the resulting dialog box, you can choose which data to include in your pivot table. For example, you might only want to include data from the past year. Filtering your data can be helpful for spotting trends that might not be immediately obvious.

Lastly, you can use Numbers' sort feature to find trends. With your pivot table selected, go to the Data menu and select "Sort." You can choose how you will sort your data in the resulting dialog box. Sorting your data by a particular field can help spot trends, such as seasonal trends. For example, you might see that sales are higher in the summer than in the winter.

Let's say you have a pivot table that shows the number of products sold by month, and you want to identify which months have seen the highest sales. Here's how each approach could be used:

- Pivot chart: You create a pivot chart and notice that sales have increased steadily over the past few months, with the highest sales occurring in the most recent month.
- Filter: You use the filter feature to only show data from the last six months, and notice that sales have been consistently high in the past two months.
- Sort: You sort the data by month and see that sales are highest in July and August, which are the summer months.

By using these methods to find trends in your data, you can gain valuable insights and make informed decisions. Pivot tables are a great tool for analyzing data, and using these features in Numbers makes it easy to spot trends that might otherwise go unnoticed.

BEST PRACTICES FOR EFFECTIVE PIVOT TABLE USAGE

While the basic steps of creating a pivot table in Numbers are relatively straightforward, there are some best practices you can follow to make your pivot tables more effective. Here are some tips for using pivot tables in Numbers:

- Start with well-organized data: Before creating a pivot table, make sure that your data is well-organized, with clear headers and consistent formatting. This will make it easier to create a pivot table that accurately reflects your data.

- Choose the right type of pivot table: There are several types of pivot tables to choose from, including table, column, row, and page. Choose the type of pivot table that best suits your needs, based on the type of data you have and the questions you want to answer.

- Use filters to refine your data: Filters allow you to limit the data displayed in your pivot table based on specific criteria. This can help you focus on a particular subset of your data, making it easier to spot trends or patterns.

- Format your pivot table: Once you have created your pivot table, take the time to format it in a way that is easy to read and understand. Use bold fonts, colors, and borders to make your pivot table stand out on the page.

- Update your pivot table regularly: If your data changes frequently, make sure to update your pivot table regularly to reflect the latest information. This will ensure that you always have the most accurate and up-to-date information.

For example, suppose you have a table that shows the sales figures for different products in different regions. By using a pivot table, you can quickly see which products are selling the most and in which regions. You could use a filter to limit the data to a specific region, or you could sort the data by product to see which products are the most popular.

TROUBLESHOOTING COMMON PIVOT TABLE ISSUES

While pivot tables in Numbers can be a powerful tool for data analysis, there can be instances where you may encounter issues. Here are some common pivot table issues you may encounter and troubleshooting tips to help resolve them:

1. Incorrect Data: If you notice that your pivot table is not displaying accurate data, double-check your source data to make sure it is correct. Additionally, check your pivot table settings to ensure they are configured properly.

2. Missing Data: If you notice that certain data is missing from your pivot table, check to make sure that the relevant columns and rows are included in your source data. Also, make sure that the field headers in your source data match the headers in your pivot table.

3. Incorrect Pivot Table Settings: If your pivot table is not displaying the data you expect, check to make sure that your pivot table settings are configured correctly. You can do this by clicking on the pivot table and checking the "Pivot Table Editor" window.

4. Data is not Refreshing: If your pivot table is not updating with new data, make sure that automatic updates are turned on. You can do this by going to the "Pivot Table Editor" and selecting "Refresh Data." You can also manually refresh your pivot table by selecting "Refresh Table" from the "Data" menu.

5. Large Data Sets: If you have a large amount of data in your pivot table, it may take longer to load or update. Consider optimizing your data by removing unnecessary columns or rows.

By troubleshooting these common pivot table issues, you can ensure that your pivot tables in Numbers are accurately displaying your data and providing valuable insights.

Organize Your Data

Make sure that your data is organized correctly. Pivot tables require that your data be organized in a specific way to work properly. If your data is not organized correctly, the pivot table will not be able to interpret it correctly.

Check for Blank Cells

Next, check to see any blank cells in your data. Blank cells can cause problems with pivot tables, so it's important to ensure that all your data is entered correctly. Finally, check your pivot table's settings to ensure everything is set up correctly. You can always contact Numbers support for help if you're still having trouble.

You should be able to troubleshoot any pivot table issues using these tips. Have fun pivoting!

FAQS ABOUT PIVOT TABLES

Q: How do I change the Pivot Table layout in Numbers?

A: To change the layout of a pivot table in Numbers, first click the Layout tab. Then use the options in the Pivot Table Layout section to specify how you want your pivot table to look. For example, you can choose whether to show or hide subtotals and grand totals, or you can choose to display data in a tabular or compact form.

Q: How do I filter data in a Pivot Table in Numbers?

A: To filter data in a pivot table in Numbers, first click the Data tab. Then use the options in the Pivot Table Data section to specify which data you want to include in your pivot table. For example, you can choose to only show data for a specific period or a specific category.

Q: How do I format a Pivot Table in Numbers?

A: First, click the Format tab to format a pivot table in Numbers. Then use the options in the Pivot Table Format section to specify how you want your pivot table to look. You can, for example, change the number format or the font style and size. You can add borders or background colors to your pivot table using the options in this section.

Q: How do I print a Pivot Table in Numbers?

A: To print a pivot table in Numbers, first click the File tab. Then select Print from the drop-down menu. Next, choose how you want your pivot table to be printed. For example, you can print only the data or the pivot table, including the field list and header. Finally, click the Print button.

CHAPTER 4: VISUALIZING DATA WITH RADAR CHARTS

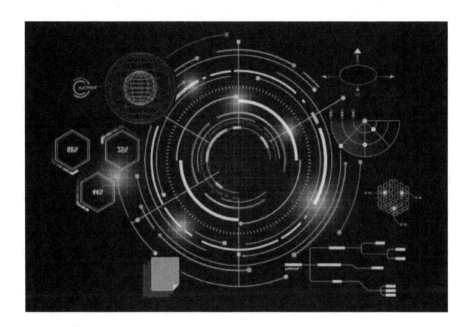

WHAT IS A RADAR CHART?

Radar charts are mainly used to compare data sets and visualize relationships between them. You can use them to show how different items in a data set relate to or compare two or more data sets.

Radar charts are composed of a series of connected lines, called radii, which originate from a common center point. The length of each line represents the value of the item to which it is connected. The lines are arranged to form a circle, or radii, with the center point in the middle.

Radar charts are a great way to see how data sets compare. You can use them to compare items in a data set or two or more data sets. Radar charts are also a good way to see relationships between different items in a data set

NUMBERS APP AND RADAR CHART

The numbers app is a powerful tool to help you create sophisticated charts and graphs. One type of chart you may want to use is a radar chart. Radar charts are useful for visualizing data that has multiple variables. For example, a radar chart can be used to compare the performance of two different athletes.

Radar charts are similar to line graphs but have a few key differences. First, radar charts show data points that are connected by lines. It makes it easy to see patterns and relationships between data points. Second, you can use radar charts to show data over time. It is helpful if you want to track an athlete's progress or compare the performance of two athletes over time.

If you're looking for a way to visualize data more sophisticatedly, consider using a radar chart in Numbers App. Radar charts can help you see relationships and patterns that you may not be able to see with other types of charts.

CREATING RADAR CHARTS IN NUMBERS

You can use radar charts to compare two or more data sets.

1. Click on the "Charts" button in the toolbar and choose "Radar" from the list of chart types.
2. A default radar chart will be created with your data. You can now customize the chart by clicking on it and using the "Chart" and "Format" tabs in the sidebar.
3. In the "Chart" tab, you can adjust settings like the chart title, data labels, and grid lines. In the "Format" tab, you can change the appearance of the chart, including colors, fonts, and the chart style.
4. If you need to add or remove data from your chart, simply select the chart and click on the "Chart Data" button in the toolbar. From there, you can add or remove data from your chart as needed.
5. Finally, you can adjust the layout of your chart by selecting it and using the green dots that appear around the chart to resize and position it on your sheet.
6. Click the Save button to save changes.

INTERPRETING RADAR CHART

Radar charts help to visualize data but can be tricky to interpret. Here are a few tips to help you make the most of your radar chart:

Look at the Overall Shape of the Data

When looking at a radar chart, the overall shape of the data is what you should focus on. It will give you an idea of the general trends and patterns in the data. Specifically, look for clusters of data points and any outlier points. These can give you insights into the factors most important to the data set.

To interpret a radar chart, start by looking at the overall shape of the data. If the data is clustered together, this indicates that there is a strong relationship between the variables. The relationship between the variables is weak if the data is spread out. You can also look at the individual data points to see any outliers.

Next, compare the different data sets on the radar chart. Look for similarities and differences in the shapes of the data sets. It can give an insight into the relationship between the variables. Finally, compare the data sets to any external data that you have. It can help you understand the data's context and see if there are any trends you can identify.

You can also compare different data sets to look for trends. Finally, you can compare the data to external data to understand the context of the data.

Pay Attention to the Axes

When reading a radar chart, it is important to pay attention to the axes. The axes represent the different variables that are being compared. The length of each line represents the value of that variable.

So, if you are looking at a radar chart comparing the average temperatures of two cities, the city with the long line would be the warmer city.

It is also necessary to pay attention to the scale of each axis. The scale will tell you how big the difference is between the two values. For example, if the scale goes from 0 to 100, then a difference of 50 would be significant, but if the scale only goes from 0 to 10, that difference of 50 would not be as substantial.

When looking at a radar chart, pay attention to the axes and the scale to interpret the data correctly.

Each axis represents a different data point, so make sure you know what each one represents. Finally, don't forget to label your axes! It will help you and others interpret the data more efficiently.

Look for Patterns in the Individual Data Points

When looking at a radar chart, you should look for patterns in the individual data points. Do any of the points form a line? Are any of the points particularly far from the others?

Once you've identified any patterns, you can start to interpret what they mean. For example, if all of the points form a line, that could indicate that the data is linear. If one point is far from the others, that could indicate an outlier.

Keep in mind that no one correct interpretation of a radar chart exists. The important thing is to look for patterns and then think about what those patterns could mean.

CUSTOMIZING RADAR CHARTS IN NUMBERS

Customizing radar charts in Numbers can help to make your data more understandable and visually appealing. Here are some ways you can customize radar charts:

1. Change the Chart Type: By default, a radar chart is set to show each data series as a line. However, you can change the chart type to show each data series as a filled shape. To do this, select the chart, go to the Format sidebar, and choose the "Chart" tab. Then, choose "Filled" from the "Line Type" drop-down menu.
2. Adjust the Scale: Depending on your data, you may need to adjust the scale of the radar chart. To do this, select the chart and go to the Format sidebar. Choose the "Axes" tab, and then choose "Primary Radial" from the drop-down menu. From there, you can adjust the minimum, maximum, and interval values for the scale.
3. Change the Data Series Colors: By default, Numbers assigns different colors to each data series in a radar chart. However, you may want to change these colors to better match your presentation or branding. To do this, select the chart and go to the Format sidebar. Choose the "Chart" tab, and then choose "Series" from the drop-down menu. From there, you can choose a new color for each data series.
4. Add Data Labels: To make your radar chart more readable, you may want to add data labels to each data point. To do this, select the chart and go to the Format sidebar. Choose the "Chart" tab, and then choose "Data Labels" from the drop-down menu. From there, you can choose to show the values or percentages for each data point.
5. Customize the Legend: By default, Numbers displays a legend for each data series in a radar chart. However, you may want to customize the legend to better match your presentation or branding. To do this, select the chart and go to the Format sidebar. Choose the "Chart" tab, and then choose

"Legend" from the drop-down menu. From there, you can customize the font, size, and position of the legend.

6. Add Gridlines: Gridlines can help to make your radar chart more readable and understandable. To add gridlines to a radar chart, select the chart and go to the Format sidebar. Choose the "Chart" tab, and then choose "Gridlines" from the drop-down menu. From there, you can choose to show or hide the gridlines, and customize the style and color of the lines.

ADVANTAGES OF USING RADAR CHARTS

Radar charts are a great way to visualize data. They can be used to show trends over time or to compare different data sets. Radar charts are also easy to read and understand, making them a valuable tool for decision-makers.

There are many advantages to using radar charts in Numbers. Here are just a few:

Radar Charts are Easy to Understand

Radar charts are easy to understand and can be a valuable tool for decision-making. They are handy for comparing data sets that have different ranges. For example, you can easily use a radar chart to compare your company's sales figures for the past year. The chart would show how each month's sales compared to the others, and you could quickly see which months were the best and worst performers.

You can also use radar charts to track progress. For example, you could track your team's sales figures month-by-month. It would allow you to see how the team performs and identify trends.

Radar charts are a great option if you're looking for a way to compare data sets and see how they relate. They're easy to understand and can be a valuable tool for decision-making.

You can use Radar Charts to Compare Different Data Sets

You can use radar charts to see how different groups of people or different types of data compare. You can use radar charts to compare anything from age groups to income levels.

Radar charts are handy for comparing data with many different variables. For example, you could use a radar chart to compare the age, income, and education level of two different groups of people.

Radar charts are also an excellent way to visualize data that changes over time. You can use them to see how a group of people's age, income, and education level have changed over time.

Radar Charts are a Valuable Tool for Decision-Makers

Radar charts in Numbers are a valuable tool for decision-makers. They provide an easy way to compare data points and make informed decisions. You can use radar charts to track progress over time, compare data sets, or make forecasts. When used correctly, radar charts can be an invaluable asset in the decision-making process.

Radar charts are created by plotting data points on a two-dimensional graph. The data points are connected to form a polygon. The shape of the polygon will vary depending on the plotted data points. You can use radar charts to track progress over time, compare data sets, or make forecasts.

When used correctly, radar charts can be an invaluable asset in the decision-making process. They provide an easy way to compare data points and make informed decisions. However, radar charts can also be misleading if not used correctly. It is crucial to understand how radar charts work before making decisions.

Radar Charts are a Great Way to Visualize Data

Radar charts are of great help in visualizing data. They can be used to show how different items compare to one another or to show how a single item changes over time.

Radar charts are created by plotting data points on a grid and then connecting the dots to create a polygon. You can use the size of the polygons to visualize the data, with larger polygons representing larger values.

These are great tools for visualizing data and showing how different items compare or how a single item changes over time.

If you're looking for a way to visualize your data better, consider using radar charts in Numbers. You'll be glad you did!

DISADVANTAGES OF USING RADAR CHARTS

Radar charts have a few disadvantages that you should consider before using them.

Difficulty in Reading

Radar charts are often criticized for being difficult to read and interpret. It is because the various data points are spread out evenly around the perimeter of the chart, making it hard to compare them side by side. In addition, the lines connecting the data points can be confusing and make it difficult to see relationships between different data sets.

Can be Misleading

Radar charts are a great way to compare data sets, but they can also be misleading. When using radar charts, it's important to remember that the data points' angles can distort the data. For example, if two data sets have the same value for one data point but different values for another, the data set with the higher value will appear further away from the center of the chart. It can be misleading, and it's essential to be aware of this when interpreting data from a radar chart.

Radar charts can also be difficult to read because all data points appear to be the same distance from the center. It is why it's often helpful to use colors or different shapes to distinguish between different data sets on a radar chart.

Not Well-Suited for Comparing More Than Two Data Sets

Radar charts are not well suited for comparing more than two data sets in Numbers. They can often be misleading when comparing three or more data sets. It is because the shape of the radar chart changes as more data sets are added, making it difficult to accurately compare the data sets' relative sizes.

Overall, radar charts are a great tool for comparing data sets, but it's essential to be aware of their limitations. If you're not careful, radar charts can be misleading. However, if you keep these things in mind, radar charts can be a great way to visualize data.

CHAPTER 5: CONVERTING HANDWRITING TO TEXT IN NUMBERS

As you may know, Numbers is a spreadsheet application part of the iWork suite of productivity applications. While it is primarily designed for working with numbers and data, it also has some great features for working with text. One of these features is the ability to turn handwriting into text.

It can be a great way to enter data into a spreadsheet if you don't have a keyboard handy or prefer to write instead of type. It can also be helpful for quickly jotting down notes or ideas.

You can use the Turning handwriting into text feature in Numbers in a few different ways. You can use it to quickly enter data into a spreadsheet or convert a handwritten note into text that you can edit.

If you're using the feature to enter data into a spreadsheet, you can write the data in the cells where you want it to appear. Handwriting recognition will convert your handwriting into text and enter it into the cell.

If you're using the feature to convert a handwritten note into editable text, you can write the note in any blank area of the Numbers document. When you're finished, tap the Convert button, and handwriting recognition will convert your handwriting into text. The text will appear in a new text box that you can move and resize as needed. You can edit the text as you would any other text in Numbers.

Turning handwriting into text can be a great way to quickly enter data into a Numbers spreadsheet or convert a handwritten note into editable text.

BENEFITS OF CONVERTING HANDWRITING TO TEXT

Here are the listed reasons why you might want to turn handwritten text into typed text in Numbers:

- You've been given a document only available in handwritten form.
- You've taken some notes by hand and want to type them up.
- You want to make your handwritten text more legible.
- You want to make searching for specific text within a handwritten document easier.
- You want to save your handwritten text as a PDF or other format.

These are valid reasons why you might want to turn handwritten text into typed text in Numbers. And luckily, doing so is a relatively simple process.

CONVERTING HANDWRITING TO TEXT WITH KEYBOARD SHORTCUTS

Converting handwriting to text is a useful feature in Numbers that can save you time and make your data more organized. One way to do this is by using keyboard shortcuts. Here's how to convert handwriting to text with keyboard shortcuts in Numbers:

1. First, open the Numbers app and select the cell that contains the handwritten text you want to convert.
2. Next, click on the cell to make it active, and then press the "Control" and "Command" keys simultaneously.
3. While holding down the "Control" and "Command" keys, tap the spacebar on your keyboard. This will open the "Dictation" tool in Numbers.
4. Once the "Dictation" tool is open, move your cursor over the handwritten text and click on it. The tool will then begin converting the handwriting to text.
5. When the conversion is complete, you can edit the text as needed.

Using keyboard shortcuts to convert handwriting to text is a quick and easy way to get your handwritten data into a digital format. With just a few keystrokes, you can have your data ready to be analyzed or shared.

CONVERTING HANDWRITING TO TEXT WITH TOUCH BAR

In Numbers for Mac, you can quickly use the Touch Bar to convert handwriting to text. Here's how:

1. First, open the Numbers app and select the cell that contains the handwritten text you want to convert.
2. Next, click on the cell to make it active, and then tap the "Input Source" button on the Touch Bar. This button looks like a globe with a pen.
3. In the input source options that appear on the Touch Bar, select "Convert to Text." This will open the "Dictation" tool in Numbers.
4. Once the "Dictation" tool is open, move your cursor over the handwritten text and click on it. The tool will then begin converting the handwriting to text.
5. When the conversion is complete, you can edit the text as needed.

The text you entered will appear in the cell. If you make a mistake, tap to delete it, then start again.

You can also use the Touch Bar to convert images of handwritten text into editable text. Here's how:

1. Open the Numbers app and select the cell that contains the image of the handwritten text you want to convert.
2. Tap on the cell to make it active, and then look for the "Convert Handwriting" button on the Touch Bar.
3. Tap on the "Convert Handwriting" button to activate the feature.
4. The Touch Bar will then display a preview of the converted text.
5. If you're satisfied with the conversion, simply click on the text preview to insert it into the cell.
6. You can then edit the text as needed.

The text you entered will appear in the cell. If you make a mistake, tap to delete it, then start again.

BEST PRACTICES FOR ACCURATE TEXT CONVERSION

The Conversion Process is not Perfect

As we all know, the conversion process is not perfect when converting handwriting to text in Numbers. Inevitably, some of the original content will be lost or changed. It can be frustrating for users who rely on this feature to convert their handwritten notes into digital text.

There are a few things you can do to improve the accuracy of the conversion process:

- **Make sure your handwriting is legible**. If the converter can't read your handwriting, it won't be able to convert it accurately.
- **Use simple language and short sentences**. The converter works best with simple language and short sentences. Avoid using abbreviations, acronyms, and jargon.
- **Use a pen with a narrow tip**. The converter works best with pens with narrow tips. Avoid using thick markers or highlighters.
- **Write on lined paper**. The converter works best when handwriting is written on lined paper. It helps the converter "read" the handwriting more accurately.
- **Take your time**. The converter works best when you take time and write slowly and clearly. Avoid writing in a hurry or in a sloppy way.

By following these tips, you can improve the accuracy of the conversion process and avoid losing or changing important information in your handwritten notes.

The Converted Text may not Match the Original Handwriting

If you're converting handwritten text to typed text in Numbers, there's a chance that the converted text may not perfectly match the original handwriting. The conversion process is imperfect, and some details may be lost in translation. However, the converted text should be accurate enough if you're looking for a general idea of the handwritten text.

Numbers Can Only Convert Handwriting to Text in English

When you convert handwriting to text in Numbers, the software can only accurately interpret and convert English text. The results may be inaccurate if you're trying to convert handwriting to another language - such as French or Spanish. The same is true for converting other languages' written characters into English text; the results may not be perfect.

CHAPTER 6: ADDING COLOR, GRADIENTS, AND IMAGES TO YOUR SPREADSHEETS

Color, gradients, and images are important design elements in Numbers. They can add visual interest and contrast to your documents, making them more engaging and visually appealing.

When incorporating color into your Numbers documents, remember a few things. First, consider the purpose of the document. Is it meant to be informational or decorative? If it's informational, you'll want to use colors that are easy to read and understand.

Second, think about the audience for the document. What types of colors will they respond best to? For example, corporate audiences may prefer more subdued colors, while creative audiences may prefer brighter, more vibrant colors.

Third, consider the overall design of the document. What colors will complement or contrast with the other elements in the document? For example, if you're using a lot of white space, you might want to use a dark color for your text to stand out. Or, if you're using many images, you might want to use a light color for your text so that it doesn't compete with the visuals.

You can also use color to convey meaning. For example, red might be used to indicate danger or urgency, while blue might be used to represent calmness or serenity. When using color in your document, be aware of the message you're trying to communicate and choose colors accordingly.

Gradients are another way to add visual interest to your Numbers documents. A gradient is a gradual transition from one color to another. You can create gradients using the built-in tools in Numbers or purchase pre-made gradient files to use in your documents.

When using gradients, keep in mind that you should use them sparingly. Too much of a gradient can make a document look busy or cluttered. Additionally, gradients can be difficult to read, so use them sparingly in text-heavy documents.

Images are another way to add visual interest to your Numbers documents. You can insert images from your computer or search for royalty-free images online.

When using images, keep in mind that you should use them sparingly. Too many images can make a document look busy or cluttered. Additionally, images can be difficult to read, so use them sparingly in text-heavy documents.

When incorporating color, gradients, and images into your Numbers documents, remember these tips to create engaging and visually appealing documents.

ADDING COLOR, GRADIENTS, AND IMAGES TO CELLS IN NUMBERS

In addition to adding text and numbers to cells, you can add color, gradients, and images. It can help make your data more visually appealing and easy to understand.

1. Select the cell or cells you want to format.
2. Click on the "Cell" tab in the Format sidebar.
3. To change the background color of the cell, click the "Fill" drop-down menu and select a color. You can also choose a gradient by selecting "Gradient Fill" and choosing a preset gradient or creating a custom one.
4. To add an image to the cell, click "Image Fill," then drag and drop an image onto the placeholder or click the "Choose" button to select an image from your files. You can also adjust the opacity and scale of the image using the options in the Image Fill section.

5. To add a border to the cell, click the "Border" drop-down menu and select a border style. You can adjust the line weight, color, and style of the border using the options in the Border section.

6. To apply the formatting to multiple cells, select the cells and click the "Paintbrush" button in the Format sidebar. Then click on the cell with the formatting you want to copy and click on the cells you want to apply it to.

APPLYING COLOR AND GRADIENT FILLS TO SHAPES IN NUMBERS

You can use color and gradient fills to add visual interest to shapes in Numbers.

1. First, select the shape you want to apply a fill to.
2. Next, click on the "Style" tab in the Format inspector.
3. From there, click on the "Fill" drop-down menu, and choose whether you want to apply a color or a gradient fill.
4. If you choose a color fill, you can either choose a preset color from the list or create a custom color by clicking on the color wheel.
5. If you choose a gradient fill, you can choose from several preset gradients or create a custom gradient by clicking on the gradient editor.
6. Once you've chosen the fill you want to apply, you can adjust the opacity and angle of the fill as desired.

By applying color and gradient fills to shapes in Numbers, you can make your spreadsheets more visually appealing and help to draw attention to important information.

INCORPORATING IMAGES INTO YOUR SPREADSHEET

Adding images to shapes in Numbers is a great way to add visual interest to your documents. Here's how:

1. Open the Numbers app on your Mac.
2. Click on the sheet that contains the shape you want to add an image to.
3. Select the shape by clicking on it.
4. From the "Inspector" panel, click on the "Graphic" tab.
5. In the "Fill" section, click on the "Image Fill" button.
6. Click on the "Choose" button and select the image file you want to use from your computer.
7. Adjust the image settings, such as the scale, position, and rotation, to fit the shape using the "Image Fill" section in the "Inspector" panel.

8. Click outside the shape to deselect it.

Once you have completed these steps, the image will be applied as a fill to the shape in your Numbers spreadsheet. By adding images to shapes, you can enhance the visual appeal of your spreadsheets and make them more engaging and informative.

ADJUSTING TRANSPARENCY AND RESIZING IMAGES

In Numbers, you can adjust the transparency and size of images to make them fit better into your spreadsheet. Here's how to do it:

Adjusting Transparency

1. First, select the image you want to adjust.
2. Click on the "Format" button in the upper-right corner of the Numbers window.
3. Click on the "Style" tab in the Format pane that appears.
4. Move the "Transparency" slider to the right to make the image more transparent, or to the left to make it less transparent.
5. Once you have set the desired level of transparency, you can close the Format pane.

Resizing Images

1. Select the image you want to resize.
2. Hover your mouse over one of the corners of the image until a double-headed arrow appears.
3. Click and drag the corner of the image to the desired size.
4. Alternatively, you can adjust the size of the image using the "Width" and "Height" fields in the "Arrange" tab of the Format pane.
5. Once you have set the desired size, you can close the Format pane.

Adjusting transparency and resizing images in Numbers can help you create more visually appealing and polished spreadsheets.

MODIFYING THE COLOR, GRADIENT, OR IMAGE OF A CELL IN NUMBERS

To modify the color, gradient, or image of a cell in Numbers, follow these steps:

1. Select the cell or cells that you want to modify.
2. In the format sidebar, click on the "Cell" tab.

3. To change the cell color, click the "Color Fill" drop-down menu and select a color. You can also use the color picker to select a custom color.

4. To apply a gradient to the cell, click the "Gradient Fill" drop-down menu and select a gradient. You can adjust the gradient direction and angle using the controls below the drop-down menu.

5. To add an image to the cell, click the "Image Fill" drop-down menu and select "Choose Image." Select an image from your files or drag and drop an image into the image well.

6. To adjust the transparency of the cell color, gradient, or image, use the "Opacity" slider under the fill options.

7. To remove the fill from the cell, select the cell and click the "No Fill" button in the format sidebar.

RESIZING AND MOVING CELLS

In Numbers, resizing and moving cells is a fundamental part of formatting and organizing your spreadsheet. Here are some steps to follow when resizing and moving cells:

Resizing Cells

1. Select the cells you want to resize. You can do this by clicking and dragging your mouse over the cells or by clicking on a specific cell and dragging the blue handle on the bottom right corner of the selection.

2. Once the cells are selected, hover your mouse over the border of the selected cells until you see a double arrow.

3. Click and drag the double arrow to resize the cells. You can resize both horizontally and vertically.

Moving Cells

1. Select the cells you want to move. You can do this by clicking and dragging your mouse over the cells or by clicking on a specific cell and dragging the blue handle on the bottom right corner of the selection.

2. Once the cells are selected, hover your mouse over the border of the selected cells until you see a four-arrow icon.

3. Click and drag the cells to their new location.

There are several keyboard shortcuts in Numbers that can be used for resizing and moving cells:

1. To move a cell or range of cells using the keyboard, first select the cells you want to move. Then, press and hold the "Option" key and use the arrow keys to move the cells in the desired direction.

2. To resize a cell or range of cells using the keyboard, first select the cells you want to resize. Then, press and hold the "Option" and "Shift" keys simultaneously. Use the arrow keys to increase or decrease the size of the cells.

3. To quickly resize a single column or row, click on the header for the column or row you want to resize. Then, press and hold the "Option" key while dragging the header to the desired size.

DELETING COLOR, GRADIENTS, AND IMAGES FROM CELLS IN NUMBERS

If you're no longer happy with the color, gradient, or image you've applied to a cell in Numbers, you can delete it by following these steps:

1. Tap the cell that contains the color, gradient, or image you want to remove.
2. In the Format sidebar, tap the Cell tab.
3. Tap the drop-down menu next to Fill and select None.
4. Tap Done to save your changes.

TROUBLESHOOTING COMMON IMAGE ISSUES

If your color, gradient, or image doesn't appear the way you expect it to in Numbers, there are a few things you can try.

First, check that your document is using the correct color profile. To do this, go to the Inspector's Document tab and ensure the Color Profile drop-down menu is set to sRGB IEC61966-2.1.

If that doesn't fix the problem, try resetting your document's colors by clicking the Document tab in the Inspector and the Reset Colors button.

If you're still having trouble, make sure that the image you're using is in an RGB color space. You can check this by opening the image in an image editing program like Photoshop and looking at the color mode. It should say RGB.

If you're still having trouble after that, try creating a new document and importing your color, gradient, or image. It will often fix any problems caused by corrupt or incompatible data.

You can also delete colors, gradients, and images from cells by selecting them and pressing the Delete key on your keyboard.

One of the most common issues people have with Numbers is getting colors, gradients, and images to display correctly in cells.

- Make sure the cell is big enough to accommodate the content. Sometimes increasing the height or width of the cell can help.
- If the cell has a lot of content, try adjusting the font size or line spacing. It can help make the content more readable.
- Make sure that the color profile of your document is set to "RGB Color" or "Generic RGB." You can change this in the "Document Info" section of the Numbers app.

CHAPTER 7: WORKING WITH SHAPES IN NUMBERS

Shapes play an essential role in the Numbers app. They help to create a visual representation of data, making it easier to understand and interpret. There are a variety of shapes available to use, each with its purpose and meaning. By understanding the different roles that shapes can play, you'll be able to use them more effectively to communicate your data.

One of the most basic uses for shapes is simply delineating different data areas. For example, you might use a rectangle to surround a group of cells representing one data category and use a different shape to surround another group representing a different category. It can help to visually separate the two data sets, making understanding the relationships between them easier.

You can also use shapes to highlight specific data points. For example, you might use a larger or brighter-colored shape to draw attention to a crucial data point. It can help ensure that your audience doesn't miss anything important.

Finally, you can use shapes to add a bit of visual interest to your Numbers document. It can help to make it more visually appealing and can also help to keep your audience engaged.

When using shapes in the Numbers app, they must remember their purpose and meaning. Doing so will allow you to use them more effectively to communicate your data.

HOW TO INSERT A SHAPE IN NUMBERS

To insert a shape in Numbers, follow these steps:

1. Tap the "+" sign at the top-right corner of the screen.
2. Select "Shape" from the menu that appears.
3. Choose the type of shape you want to insert from the options that appear.
4. Tap and drag your finger to place the shape where you want it on the screen.
5. Tap "Done" when you're finished.

HOW TO CHANGE THE COLOR OF A SHAPE IN NUMBERS

To change the color of a shape in Numbers, do the following:

1. Select the shape you want to change.
2. In the "Format" panel, click on the "Fill" tab.
3. Choose the color you want from the palette.
4. Click "OK" to save your changes.

You can also change the color of a shape by selecting it and then clicking on the "Fill" color swatch in the "Format" panel. It will open the color picker, where you can choose a new color. Click "OK" to save your changes.

HOW TO DELETE A SHAPE

The first way is to select the shape and press the "delete" button on your keyboard. You can right-click or two-finger tap on the shape and select "delete" from the menu that appears as well.

If you want to delete multiple shapes at once, you can select them all. While clicking on each shape, simply hold down the "shift" key. Then, you can press the "delete" button or right-click and select "delete" from the menu.

You can also delete a shape by selecting it and then clicking on the trashcan icon at the screen's top.

UTILIZING THE SHAPES LIBRARY ON MOBILE DEVICES

To use shapes in Numbers on an iPhone or iPad, select the cell you want to insert a shape into. Then tap the "Shapes" icon in the toolbar at the top of the screen.

It will open up the shapes library, which contains various shapes you can insert into your spreadsheet. To insert a shape, tap on it.

You can also resize and move shapes after they've been inserted by tapping on them and then using the handles that appear. And if you need to delete a shape, tap on it and then hit the "Delete" button.

That's all there is to using shapes in Numbers! With this handy tool, you can make your spreadsheets much more visually appealing and easier to understand. So, experiment with different shapes to see what works best for your needs.

CHAPTER 8: UNDERSTANDING FUNCTIONS IN NUMBERS

Functions play a vital role in the Numbers app. By allowing users to group and manipulate data, functions give users greater control over their work. In addition, you can use functions to automate tasks, making it easier and faster to complete work.

Whether you are looking to organize your data or automate a task, the Numbers app has a function that can help. To learn more about the role of functions in Numbers, read on.

As previously mentioned, you can use functions to sort and manipulate data. It is done by creating a function formula, which is then applied to a range of cells. For example, you could use a function to sum a column of numbers or count the number of cells that contain a certain value.

You can also use functions to automate tasks. For example, you could use a function to automatically insert the current date into a cell or calculate the average of a range of cells. By automating tasks, you can save time and reduce errors.

Although functions are immensely powerful, they are not always necessary. Sometimes, completing a task may be easier and faster without a function. For example, if you only need to sum a column of numbers once, you may not need to create a function formula.

When deciding to use a function, consider the following:

- How often will the task be completed? If the task is going to be completed once, a function may not be necessary.
- How complex is the task? If the task is quite simple, a function may not be necessary.
- How much time do you have to complete the task? A function may not be necessary if you only have a few minutes to complete the task.

In general, functions should be used when they will save time or reduce errors. When in doubt, err on the side of using a function. The role of functions in Numbers is to save time and reduce errors. When deciding about using a function, consider the task at hand and how you could complete it more efficiently with a function.

TYPES OF FUNCTIONS

There are many types of functions in the Numbers app. You can use these functions to perform mathematical operations, convert units, and more. Here are some common types of functions in Numbers app:

- Basic Math Functions: These functions are used for simple math calculations and include addition (+), subtraction (-), multiplication (*), and division (/).
- Statistical Functions: These functions are used to analyze and summarize large sets of data and include functions like SUM, AVERAGE, MEDIAN, and MODE.
- Financial Functions: These functions are used to perform financial calculations and include functions like PV (present value), FV (future value), NPV (net present value), and IRR (internal rate of return).
- Date and Time Functions: These functions are used to manipulate and analyze dates and times and include functions like NOW, TODAY, MONTH, and YEAR.
- Text Functions: These functions are used to manipulate and format text and include functions like CONCATENATE, LEFT, RIGHT, and MID.
- Lookup and Reference Functions: These functions are used to search and reference data in a table or range of cells and include functions like VLOOKUP, HLOOKUP, INDEX, and MATCH.

- Logical Functions: These functions are used to evaluate logical expressions and include functions like IF, AND, OR, and NOT.
- Engineering Functions: These functions are used for complex engineering calculations and include functions like CONVERT, ABS, and SQRT.

To use a function in Numbers, you typically type the function name followed by its arguments. For example, to add two numbers, you can use the SUM function and type "=SUM(5, 10)" into a cell.

For conversion functions, like "CONVERT(mi, km)", you would specify the value you want to convert and the units you want to convert from and to. For example, to convert 10 miles to kilometers, you would use the CONVERT function and type "=CONVERT(10, "mi", "km")" into a cell.

You can find a full list of functions in the Numbers app by tapping the "Functions" button in the toolbar. It will open up a menu with all of the available functions. Tap on the function you want to use and enter the values you want to use.

USING FUNCTIONS IN NUMBERS FORMULAS

Functions are a powerful tool in Numbers that allow you to perform calculations and operations on your data. To use functions in Numbers formulas, follow these steps:

1. Select the cell where you want to enter your formula.
2. Begin your formula with an equal sign (=).
3. Type the name of the function you want to use, followed by an open parenthesis.
4. Enter the arguments for the function, separated by commas. The arguments are the values that the function will operate on.
5. Close the parenthesis and press Enter to complete the formula.

Here are some examples of common functions and their syntax:

1. SUM: Adds a range of numbers. Syntax: =SUM(number1:number2)
2. AVERAGE: Calculates the average of a range of numbers. Syntax: =AVERAGE(number1:number2)
3. COUNT: Counts the number of cells in a range that contain numerical data. Syntax: =COUNT(range)

Example: Suppose you have a spreadsheet that contains a list of products sold in a store, and you want to know how many of these products cost more than $50. You can use the COUNT function to count the number of cells in a given range that contain values greater than $50.

1) First, select a blank cell where you want to display the count result.

2) Then, enter the COUNT function by typing "=COUNT(" in the cell.

3) Now, select the range of cells that contain the product prices.

4) Enter the condition for the COUNT function, in this case ">50".

5) Close the parentheses and press Enter.

The formula will look something like this: =COUNT(A2:A10,">50")

This will count the number of cells in the range A2 to A10 that contain values greater than $50.

4. MAX: Returns the maximum value in a range of numbers. Syntax: =MAX(number1:number2)

Example: Suppose you have a list of numbers in cells A1 through A10, and you want to find the highest value in that range. You can use the MAX function to do this. Simply select an empty cell (let's say B1) and enter the following formula:

1) =MAX(A1:A10)

This formula tells Numbers to find the highest value in the range A1 to A10 and display it in cell B1. If the highest value is in cell A3 (let's say the value is 100), then cell B1 will display "100".

5. MIN: Returns the minimum value in a range of numbers. Syntax: =MIN(number1:number2)

Example: Let's say we have a table of sales data, with the total sales for each month in a column. We can use the MIN function to find the lowest sales number for the year. Here's how:

1) Select the cell where you want the result to appear.

2) Type "=MIN(" (without the quotes) into the cell.

3) Select the range of cells you want to find the minimum value for. In this case, we would select the column with the sales data.

4) Type ")" (without the quotes) and press Enter.

6. IF: Evaluates a condition and returns one value if the condition is true and another value if it is false. Syntax: =IF(condition, value_if_true, value_if_false).

Example: Suppose you have a list of test scores for a group of students, and you want to flag any scores that are below a certain threshold. You could use the IF function to create a new column that indicates whether each score is "Pass" or "Fail".

1) First, create a new column next to the column containing the test scores. You can do this by right-clicking on the column header and selecting "Insert Left" or "Insert Right".

2) In the first cell of the new column, type the following formula:

3) =IF(B2>=70,"Pass","Fail") This formula checks the value in cell B2 (assuming that's where the first test score is) and returns "Pass" if the score is 70 or higher, and "Fail" if it's below 70.

4) Copy the formula down the entire column to apply it to all of the test scores.

By using these and other functions, you can perform complex calculations and manipulate your data in a variety of ways. Remember to always check the syntax of a function to ensure that you are using it correctly.

CHAPTER 9: PRECISE OBJECT EDITING

Precise object editing in Numbers is a great way to ensure that your data is accurate and up-to-date. You can use it to edit objects such as cells, ranges, columns, and rows. Precise object editing can help you correct errors in your data or add new information.

When you intend to precise the object edit in Numbers, you can select the object you want to edit. It can be helpful if you need to make a small change to your data or if you want to add new information. For example, if you wanted to add a new row of data, you could use precise object editing to select the cells in the row and then enter the new data.

Precise object editing can also be helpful when you are working with large amounts of data. If you need to change many cells, you can use precise object editing to select all the cells you want to change. It can save you time and ensure that you don't accidentally make changes to other cells in your data.

If you are working with sensitive data, precise object editing can help you protect your information. You can use it to select the cells that contain sensitive data and then lock them. It will prevent others from being able to view or change the data in those cells.

Precise object editing is a powerful tool to help you manage your data more effectively. You can use it to make small changes or add new information. You can also use it to protect sensitive data. If you are not already using precise object editing in Numbers, you should consider doing so. It can save you time and ensure that your data is accurate and up-to-date.

HOW TO USE PRECISE OBJECT EDITING

With Precise object editing in Numbers, you can quickly and easily adjust the size, shape, and position of objects on your canvas. This feature is handy when working with complex designs or laying out pages for Print.

To use Precise object editing:

1. First, select the object you want to edit. You can select an object by clicking on it or by using the Shift key to select multiple objects.
2. Once you've selected your object, go to the "Format" tab in the Numbers toolbar. Here, you will see a section called "Object Styles." Click on the arrow next to "Object Styles" to open a drop-down menu.
3. From the drop-down menu, select "More." This will open the "Style" window.
4. In the "Style" window, you will see a variety of options for editing your object, including "Layout," "Borders," "Shadow," and "Reflection." You can use these options to customize the appearance of your object.
5. To make precise edits to your object, click on the "Size and Position" tab in the "Style" window. Here, you will see options for adjusting the object's position, size, rotation, and scale.
6. Use the sliders and input fields to make precise adjustments to your object. You can also use the arrow keys on your keyboard to make small adjustments to the object's position and size.
7. Once you're happy with your changes, click "OK" to apply the new styles to your object.

When you're working with objects in Precise object editing mode, you can also use the following features:

- **Duplicate an object:** Tap the Duplicate button, then tap the duplicate object to move it.
- **Delete an object:** Tap the Delete button.
- **Bring an object forward or send it backward:** Tap the Arrange button and then Bring Forward or Send Backward.
- **Lock an object in place:** Tap the Lock button. Locked objects can't be moved or edited.
- **Group multiple objects:** Tap the Group button, then tap the objects you want to group. To Ungroup objects, tap the Ungroup button.

Precise object editing is a great way to fine-tune your designs in Numbers. Give it a try the next time you're working on a complex project!

ACCESSING THE PRECISE OBJECT EDITING IN NUMBERS

To access the Precise Object Editing feature in Numbers, follow these steps:

1. Open the Numbers app and create or open a document containing an object that you want to edit.
2. Select the object by clicking on it once. The object will be surrounded by a blue outline when it is selected.
3. With the object still selected, click on the "Arrange" button in the top-right corner of the window.
4. In the drop-down menu that appears, select "Precise Object Editing" near the bottom of the list.

You can also adjust the object's position and size numerically by entering values into the Inspector pane on the right-hand side of the screen. To do this, click on the "Inspector" button in the top-right corner of the window, and then select the "Metrics" tab. Here, you can enter precise measurements for the object's size, position, and rotation.

CHAPTER 10: CREATING CAPTIONS AND TITLES

There are two types of text in Numbers: captions and titles. Captions are the labels you see on the left side of the interface, such as "Name" or "Total." Titles are headers at the top of each column, such as "January" or "Q1."

You can add or edit captions and titles by double-clicking on them. It will open up a text editor where you can make your changes.

There are a few things to keep in mind when working with captions and titles:

- Captions are typically used for labeling data, while titles are used for organizing data.
- You can use both captions and titles to sort and filter your data.
- Captions and titles can be different lengths, but they will always be the same width on the screen.
- You can use HTML tags in captions and titles to format your text. For example, you can use the <b> tag to make the text bold or the <i> tag to make the text italic.

In general, it's a good idea to keep your captions and titles short so they're easy to read.

ADDING CAPTIONS AND TITLES

Adding captions and titles to your Numbers spreadsheets can help organize and present your data clearly and professionally. Plus, it can make working with large amounts of data much easier. Here's how to add captions and titles in Numbers:

1. First, select the cell where you want to add the caption or title.
2. Next, click on the "Cell" tab in the top menu, and then select "Table" from the dropdown menu.
3. From the Table menu, select "Add Header Row" or "Add Footer Row," depending on where you want your caption or title to appear.
4. Once you've added the header or footer row, you can type in your caption or title. You can also format the text to make it more readable by selecting it and using the formatting options in the top menu.
5. If you want to add an image to your caption or title, click on the "Media" button in the top menu and select "Choose." From there, you can select an image from your computer or other device.
6. Click "OK."

Your caption or title will now appear above or below your selected cells.

EDITING CAPTIONS AND TITLES

If you're working with a Numbers spreadsheet that contains a lot of data, you may want to edit the captions and titles to make the data more easily understandable. Here's how:

1. Select the cell that you intend to edit.
2. Click the "Edit" button in the toolbar.
3. Click the "Captions & Titles" button in the editing menu.
4. Make your changes in the "Captions & Titles" dialogue box.
5. Click the "OK" button to save your changes.

You can also format your captions and titles using the "Captions & Titles" dialogue box. To do this, select the cells you want to format and click the "Format" button in the dialogue box. You can choose how you want your captions and titles to be formatted.

Captions and titles can be a great way to make your Numbers spreadsheets more understandable. By editing them, you can ensure that your data is easy to read and comprehend.

DELETING CAPTIONS AND TITLES

To delete a caption or title in Numbers:

1. Click on the text box containing the caption or title you want to delete.
2. Press the Delete key on your keyboard or right-click on the text box and select "Delete" from the context menu.
3. If you want to delete all captions or titles in your document, use the "Find" and "Replace" feature to search for the specific text and delete it.

Note: If you want to temporarily hide a caption or title without deleting it, you can simply select the text box and press the "H" key on your keyboard to hide it. To unhide the text, press "H" again.

CHAPTER 11: INCORPORATING AUDIO INTO YOUR SPREADSHEETS

A dding audio to Numbers can help bring your data to life and make it more engaging for your audience. Audio can also be a great way to add accessibility for those who may not be able to see your data or who prefer to listen rather than read.

WAYS TO ADD AUDIO

There are several ways to add audio to your spreadsheets in Numbers. One way is to use the Media Browser. You can find the Media Browser in the toolbar at the top of the Numbers window. To use the Media Browser, simply drag and drop an audio file into your document. The Media Browser will automatically insert the audio file into your document.

Another way to add audio is to use the Audio Recorder. To access this feature, select the cell where you want to add the audio and click the "Audio" button in the toolbar. From there, you can choose to record audio using your computer's microphone. Once you've finished recording, the audio will be inserted into your document.

The third way to add audio is to use the Audio Inspector. The Audio Inspector can be found in the toolbar at the top of the Numbers window. To use it, select an audio file in your document and click on the Inspector button in the toolbar. You'll see options for playback, volume, and looping in the Inspector window.

Adding audio to your spreadsheets can help make them more engaging and accessible for your audience. Whether you choose to use the Media Browser, Audio Recorder, or Audio Inspector, adding audio is a simple process in Numbers.

ADDING AUDIO TO YOUR NUMBERS SPREADSHEET

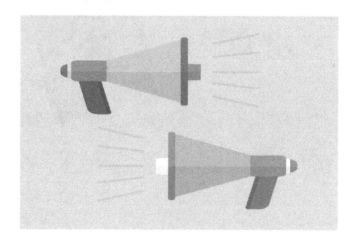

You can add audio to your Numbers spreadsheet by inserting an audio file from your computer or using the built-in microphone to record audio directly into the spreadsheet.

To Insert an Audio File:

1. Click on the cell where you want to insert the audio file.
2. Click the Insert menu and select audio.
3. Select the audio file you intend to insert and click Open.
4. You will then insert the audio file into the spreadsheet.

To record audio directly into the spreadsheet:

1. Click on the cell where you want to insert the audio recording.
2. Click the Insert menu and select audio.

3. Click the Record button.
4. Start speaking into the microphone.
5. Select the Stop button once you're done recording.
6. You will then insert the Audio Recording into the spreadsheet.

HOW TO ADD AN AUDIO FILE FROM YOUR COMPUTER IN NUMBERS

1. Click on the cell where you want to insert the audio file.
2. Go to the "Insert" menu at the top of the screen.
3. Select "Audio" from the dropdown menu.
4. In the file browser window that appears, navigate to the location of the audio file you want to insert and select it.
5. Click "Open" to insert the audio file into the selected cell.

HOW TO ADD AN AUDIO FILE FROM THE WEB

To add an audio file from the web in Numbers, first, open the Numbers app and click on the Media Browser icon in the toolbar. In the Media Browser window, select the Audio tab and search for the audio file you want to add. Once you find the audio file, click on it and then click on the "Add" button. This will add the audio file to your Numbers document.

To listen to the audio file, click on the "Play" button, or right-click on the audio file and select "save as" to download it to your computer. You can also add the audio file to your iTunes library to listen to it on your iPod or iPhone. With these simple steps, you can easily add audio files from the web to your Numbers spreadsheets.

HOW TO ADD AN AUDIO FILE FROM YOUR IOS DEVICE

Audio files from your iOS device can be added to Numbers spreadsheets in two ways: via the media browser or by using the share sheet.

To add an audio file from the media browser:

1. Tap the "+" button at the screen's top-left corner.
2. Select "Media" from the list of options.
3. Tap "Audio" in the media browser.
4. Select the audio file you wish to add.

To add an audio file using the share sheet:

1. Tap the "+" button at the top-left corner of the screen.
2. Select "Share Sheet" from the list of options.
3. Tap "Audio" in the share sheet.
4. Select the audio file you wish to add.

Adding audio files from your iOS device is a great way to enhance your Numbers spreadsheets. Whether you're adding sound effects to a game or want to include a musical accompaniment, audio files can add an extra level of interest and engagement.

HOW TO RECORD AN AUDIO FILE IN NUMBERS

Now that you know how to set up your audio recording device in Numbers, it's time to learn how to record an audio file.

1. To record an audio file in Numbers, open the Audio Recorder window by clicking on the "Audio Recorder" button in the toolbar.
2. First, ensure that the "Input" drop-down menu is set to the audio input device you want to use. Afterward, select the "Record" button to start recording.
3. You can stop recording anytime by clicking on the "Stop" button. Once you're finished recording, you can click on the "Play" button to listen back to your recording.

That's all there is to it! Now you know how to record an audio file in Numbers.

HOW TO EDIT AN AUDIO FILE

If you have an audio file you need to edit, there are a few different ways you can do so in Numbers. Here's a look at how to get started:

1. Open the Numbers file that contains the audio file.
2. Select the audio file by clicking on it once.
3. Select the "Edit" button in the toolbar.
4. Make your edits to the audio file.
5. Click on the "Save" button to save your changes.

HOW TO DELETE AN AUDIO FILE

Deleting an audio file from Numbers is simple. Just follow these steps:

1. Open the Numbers document that contains the audio file you want to delete.
2. Select the audio file by clicking on it once.
3. Press the "Delete" key on your keyboard. The audio file will be deleted from the Numbers document.

CHAPTER 12: CUSTOM TEMPLATES IN NUMBERS

Numbers offers a wide variety of custom templates that you can use to create beautiful spreadsheets. Whether you need to track your finances, manage a small business, or keep tabs on a large corporation, there's a Numbers template to suit your needs.

To find the perfect template for your needs, browse the available options. You can filter templates by category or search for a specific template by name.

If you're satisfied with the template, download it and start entering your information. Numbers make it easy to input data, add formulas, and customize the appearance of your spreadsheet. With a little effort, you can create a professional-looking document that will impress your boss or clients.

So, what are you waiting for? Start browsing Numbers templates today and see how easy it is to create beautiful spreadsheets in Numbers.

CREATING A CUSTOM TEMPLATE

Creating a custom template in Numbers is easy and only requires a few simple steps. Here's how you can create your own custom template in Numbers:

1. Open Numbers on your Mac.
2. Click on the "File" menu in the top left corner of the screen and select "New Template".
3. Choose the type of template you want to create, such as a "Blank" or "Personal Budget" template.
4. Customize the template to fit your needs by adding tables, charts, and text boxes.
5. Once you've finished creating your template, click on the "File" menu and select "Save as Template".
6. Enter a name for your custom template and click "Save".

Your custom template will now be saved and accessible from the "My Templates" section of the template chooser.

Creating a custom template in Numbers can save you time and make your workflow more efficient. By customizing your own template, you can ensure that your spreadsheets are always set up the way you need them to be.

SAVING A CUSTOM TEMPLATE IN NUMBERS

If you've created a custom template in Numbers that you want to save for future use, follow these steps.

1. Select the template you want to save from the Template Chooser.
2. Click the Save as Template button in the lower-left corner of the Template Chooser.
3. Enter a name for your template, then click Save.

It will now save your custom template in the My Templates section of the Template Chooser for future use.

ACCESSING CUSTOM TEMPLATES

Select the "Templates" tab from the Numbers home screen to access custom templates in Numbers. You can browse through a selection of custom templates or search for a specific template by keyword. Once you've found the perfect template for your needs, click on it to open it up in the Numbers interface.

You can also access custom templates in Numbers by selecting "File" > "New from Template..." from the menu bar. It will open a Finder window where you can browse your template library. Select the template you want to use and click "Open" to open it in Numbers.

EDITING A CUSTOM TEMPLATE

Once you've created a custom template in Numbers, you can edit it to change the look and feel of your document. To edit a custom template:

1. Open Numbers and select the template you want to edit from the Templates browser.
2. Click the Edit button in the toolbar.
3. Make changes to the template, such as adding or removing elements, changing colors or fonts, etc.
4. When you're finished, click the Save button in the toolbar.

Your changes will be saved to the template and will be applied to any new documents created from it. If you want to revert to the original version of the template, you can click the Revert to Original button in the toolbar.

DELETING A CUSTOM TEMPLATE

1. In the Numbers app, open the spreadsheet that contains the custom template you want to delete.
2. Tap the "More" button in the top-right corner of the screen.
3. Scroll down and tap "Manage Custom Templates."
4. Tap the "Delete" button next to the template you want to delete.
5. Tap "Delete Template" to confirm.

Custom templates can be a great way to save time when creating new documents in Numbers. However, if you no longer need a particular template, you can delete it from your library using the steps described above. It will ensure that your template library only contains the templates you need.

CHAPTER 13: MISCELLANEOUS FEATURES

Numbers has a number of miscellaneous features that allow you to work with a variety of file formats, import images, and add files to your spreadsheet. Here are some of the key features:

1. **Importing files:** You can import Microsoft Excel spreadsheets, Comma Separated Values (CSV), and tab-delimited text files into Numbers from your Mac or a Windows PC. You can also import Numbers '09 spreadsheets, CSV files, and tab-delimited text files on an iPad.

2. **Editing Excel files:** You can open a Numbers spreadsheet in Excel and edit it like any other Excel file. To do this, open the Numbers spreadsheet in Numbers, then choose File > Export To > Microsoft Excel.

3. **Converting to other file formats:** If you want to edit the Numbers spreadsheet in another application, such as Google Sheets, you can first convert it to a different file format. To do this, open the Numbers spreadsheet in Numbers, choose File > Export To > CSV, and then open the CSV file in the other application. You can also import Apple Pages, Microsoft Word, and Rich Text Format (RTF) files into Numbers on a Mac. To do this, open the document in the other application, choose File > Export To > Numbers, and then open the file in Numbers. Using Numbers on an iPad, you can also import Apple Pages documents and Rich Text Format (RTF) files. To do this, open the document in the other application, choose File > Share > Send Copy As PDF, and then open the file in Numbers.

4. **Importing images:** You can import photos and images from your Photos library or another app, such as Google Drive or Dropbox. To do this, open the image in the other app, choose File > Share > Send Copy As PDF, and then open the file in Numbers. You can add images to a Numbers spreadsheet by dragging them from the Photos app or another app into a cell. To do this, touch and hold the image until the menu appears, then drag the image to the cell.

5. **Adding files:** Using Numbers on a Mac, you can add files from your iCloud Drive or another cloud storage service, such as Google Drive or Dropbox. To do this, open the file in the other app, choose File > Share > Send Copy As PDF, and then open the file in Numbers. If you're using Numbers on an iPad, you can add files from iCloud Drive or another cloud storage service by opening the file in the other app, choosing File > Share > Send Copy As PDF, and then opening the file in Numbers. You can add files to a Numbers spreadsheet by dragging them into a cell from the iCloud Drive app or another app. To do this, touch and hold the file until the menu appears, then drag the file to the cell.

With these miscellaneous features, Numbers allows you to work with a variety of file formats and import images and files, making it a versatile tool for creating and managing spreadsheets.

CHAPTER 14: BENEFITS OF USING NUMBERS FOR BEGINNERS

If you're new to the Numbers app for Apple, you may be wondering what all the fuss is about. After all, there are plenty of other spreadsheet apps out there. So, what makes Numbers stand out?

Here are some benefits that Numbers offer:

EASE OF USE AND VERSATILITY

Several things make the Number App for Apple easy to use. First, it is straightforward to navigate. The interface is uncluttered and clean, so you won't be overwhelmed with options or features. Second, the app provides clear instructions on how to use its various features. And third, it offers a variety of helpful tutorials that show you how to get the most out of the app.

Overall, if you're searching for a simple-to-use app to keep you organized and on top of your finances, the Number App for Apple is a great option.

The Numbers App for Apple is a versatile tool for various purposes. Whether you need to quickly add up a bill, calculate the tip at a restaurant, or calculate the amount of change you should receive after purchasing an item - this app can do it all! It can be used for various chores, from tracking your finances to creating a budget, organizing your schedule, and managing a project.

COMPATIBILITY WITH OTHER APPLE PRODUCTS

If you're already using other Apple products like the iPhone and iPad, you'll be pleased to know that Numbers is compatible with them.

It means you can easily share files and data between your devices.

UNIQUE FEATURES AND AFFORDABILITY

Despite its simplicity, Numbers is still a powerful spreadsheet app. It includes every capability you might possibly need to do the task, including support for complex formulas, data visualization tools, and more.

Numbers are worth considering if you're looking for a budget-friendly option. It's much cheaper than comparable apps like Microsoft Excel, yet it still offers all the features you need to get the job done.

GREAT FOR BEGINNERS

The Numbers app for Apple is an excellent tool for beginners who want to manage their finances. Using it makes it easy to track your spending, budget for upcoming expenses, and see where your money goes each month. You can also use the Numbers app to create charts and graphs to visualize your financial data. The best part about the Numbers app is that it's free to download and use.

HANDLING FINANCES

The Numbers app for Apple is an excellent option if you're looking for a better way to handle your finances. Numbers can help you track your spending, budget for upcoming expenses, and see where your money goes each month. Plus, the Numbers app makes it easy to create charts and graphs to visualize your financial data. And best of all, the Numbers app is free to download and use.

Whether a complete beginner or a seasoned pro, Numbers is an excellent option for anyone needing a powerful and versatile spreadsheet app.

CHAPTER 15: TIPS FOR EFFECTIVE USE OF NUMBERS

You can do a few things to ensure you use the Numbers App for Apple effectively. Here are some tips:

USE TEMPLATES

When you open the Numbers app, you'll see a variety of templates to choose from. Beautiful spreadsheets can be quickly created using these templates. To use a template, tap on it and then enter your data. The template will automatically format everything for you.

There are templates for various purposes, including budgets, invoices, and more. And if you can't find what you're looking for, you can always create your custom template.

ORGANIZE YOUR DATA

Sort your data based on what makes sense to you. This will make it easier to find and use when you need it.

USE KEYBOARD SHORTCUTS

This can help you work more efficiently by reducing the need to constantly switch between the mouse and keyboard. For example, you can use shortcuts to quickly insert rows or columns, or to apply formatting to cells.

Here are few shortcuts:

- Command-N: Create a new spreadsheet.
- Command-O: Open an existing spreadsheet.
- Command-S: Save the current spreadsheet.
- Command-P: Print the current spreadsheet.
- Command-F: Search within the current spreadsheet.
- Command-Z: Undo the last action.
- Command-Y: Redo the last undone action.
- Command-X: Cut the selected cells, rows, or columns.
- Command-C: Copy the selected cells, rows, or columns.
- Command-V: Paste the cut or copied cells, rows, or columns.
- Command-A: Select all cells in the current spreadsheet.
- Command-B: Bold the selected text.
- Command-I: Italicize the selected text.
- Command-U: Underline the selected text.
- Command-T: Open the Fonts panel to format the selected text.
- Command-1: Open the Format panel to format the selected cells, rows, or columns.
- Command-2: Open the Table panel to format the current table.
- Command-3: Open the Chart panel to format the current chart.
- Command-4: Open the Inspector to customize object properties.
- Command-5: Show or hide the Media browser.
- Command-6: Show or hide the Comments pane.
- Command-7: Show or hide the Table of Contents pane.
- Command-8: Show or hide the Layout pane.

- Command-9: Show or hide the Find and Replace pane.
- Control-Tab: Switch between open spreadsheets.

USE FORMULAS

The app includes a variety of built-in formulas that you can use to perform calculations on your data. Be sure to take advantage of this feature to save time and energy.

USE CHARTS AND GRAPHS

The app also includes several built-in charts and graphs that you can use to visualize your data. Understanding trends and identifying relationships between different data points can be helpful.

SHARE YOUR WORK

The app includes several options to share your work with others. It can be helpful if you're working on a project collaboratively or want to share your results with others.

These pointers will aid you in getting the most out of the Numbers App for Apple and following them will make your experience with the app more efficient and effective.

CONCLUSION

The Numbers app from Apple is a powerful tool for managing data and performing calculations. With its easy-to-use interface, you can quickly input data and perform various mathematical operations. In addition, the app provides a wide range of features that allow you to customize your experience. Whether you're looking to create simple spreadsheets or complex financial models, the Numbers app can help you get the job done.

The Numbers app makes it easy to input data into your spreadsheet. To do so, tap on a cell and start typing. Also, you can use the app's built-in keyboard shortcuts to enter data quickly. For example, pressing the "Tab" key will move you to the next cell, while pressing "Enter" will create a new row.

After entering your data, you can use the Numbers app to perform various calculations. To do so, tap on a cell and select the "Formula" option. You can choose from various pre-defined formulas or create your custom ones. Once you have entered your formula, the app will automatically calculate the results and display them in the cell.

The Numbers app provides several features that allow you to customize your experience. For example, you can change the cells' font, size, and color to better suit your needs. You can add images and charts to your spreadsheet to make it visually appealing. In addition, the app provides several templates that you can use to create professional-looking spreadsheets quickly.

Whether you're looking to create simple spreadsheets or complex financial models, the Numbers app from Apple can help you get the job done. With its easy-to-use interface and excellent features, you'll be able to input data, perform calculations, and customize your experience to suit your needs more.

To conclude, the Numbers app for Apple is an excellent tool for managing and analyzing data. It is easy to use and has various features that make it a valuable asset for businesses and individuals. The Numbers app is worth considering if you are looking for a reliable and user-friendly app to help with all your data management needs.

KEYNOTE
FOR BEGINNERS

The Most Updated Crash Course to Keynote |
Learn How to Create an Impressive
Presentation in 7 Days or Less

ANDREW BLAKE

INTRODUCTION

Keynote is a powerful software that is free if you own a Mac. You've probably used PowerPoint for most of your life. But have no fear; this guide will assist you! It teaches you the fundamentals so you don't have to waste time learning hundreds of Keynote features you won't ever need. You'll be making visually stunning presentations in no time!

The world has learned that Apple's way of doing things is frequently the best. Apple and its products are synonymous with simplicity, form and function, and unparalleled user-friendliness. You already know that Apple is without a doubt the leader in the computing business when it comes to fostering an environment that encourages innovation. Indeed, Apple could channel its collective software genius into developing a better way to perform these tasks—an Apple way, right?

Apple has always been perceived as "anti-Microsoft," so some people were put off when they first introduced their suite of productivity apps, iWork. Hardcore Microsoft Office users scoffed at the idea of using Apple software to meet their productivity needs, while others tried it but didn't like it, preferring to do things the old way. However, as Apple began including the iWork apps (Pages, Keynote, and Numbers) with every Mac purchased, many people started to use and prefer them. The app interfaces were significantly more user-friendly than Microsoft's, and if you knew how to use one of them, you could pick up the others quickly.

Another exciting development that made the iWork apps more accessible to new users was the creation of iPad versions of them. As the iPad gained popularity among businesses, so did Apple's productivity apps.

Pages, Keynote, and Numbers were not compatible between OS X (Mac) and iOS (iPad), but any compatibility was better than none. Apple updated and released new versions of its iWork apps in 2013, and compatibility between the OS X and iOS versions was a top priority. As a result, Apple has completed the productivity circle, making this productivity method the most straightforward and intuitive on the market.

I hope this book will become your go-to resource for learning about Keynote and that you'll soon be spreading the word about the Apple way of doing things. Let's get started!

CHAPTER 1: KEYNOTE BASICS

Many of us, especially those who have worked in the business world for some time, have developed the notion that something simple cannot be as excellent as something absurdly and mockingly complex - this can be the result of highly successful marketing campaigns. However, Keynote provides the kind of elegant simplicity that PowerPoint has sought since the beginning of time but has yet to achieve simply because it can't shake itself free from the mayhem that is its legacy and interface.

Since Keynote has been the only usable presentation app on the iPad since its launch in 2010, iPads are incredibly popular in the business world. However, Keynote's popularity isn't limited to the business world; the more creative among us are also recognizing its capabilities and reaping the benefits of its presentation prowess. Again, the creative mind is drawn to Keynote because of its simplicity and power. I don't mean simplistic or dumbed-down, but rather the opposite. The simplicity I'm referring to is Apple's ability to cram so much power into such a small, easy-to-use, beautifully crafted, and intuitive interface.

Apple recently updated its iWork productivity suite with useful new features and tweaks that make the apps easier to use. Precise editing options in the Arrange Inspector are now available, especially in the iOS apps, to make it simpler to polish projects without a Mac.

Some instances of what you can do with Keynote are:

- PowerPoint presentations can be easily imported and exported.
- Use the included Apple-designed themes to jump-start your presentation or start from scratch and create your own impressive "preso" (cool business lingo for presentation).
- The format panel organizes all the tools you'll need to build your presentation, so you don't have to go menu hopping to get it just right. Keynote's coaching tips, like Pages', provide on-the-fly instruction and direction.
- Emphasis builds, which are subtle but eye-catching animations, highlight important objects in your presentations without detracting from your main message.
- The Presenter Display feature gives you simple and intuitive control over your presentation while keeping your audience in the dark.
- Even the most bored onlooker will be wowed by interactive charts, giving your presentation a little SNAP that draws attention to your points.
- Sending a link to a presentation via Facebook, Twitter, Messages, or Mail (Apple's messaging app, native to both OS X and iOS), the default email client for both OS X and iOS, is the easiest way to share it with others.

If you own a Mac, iPad, or iPhone, you have a third, increasingly popular option: Keynote. Keynote is free with Apple devices and is both simple and visually stunning. Even with limited knowledge of the software, it's relatively simple to get started. This guide will assist you if you want to get the most out of it. It will show you the ropes, including how to do everything you're used to in Microsoft PowerPoint and some features you might not know.

The following updates have been made to the iOS iWork apps, according to the release notes:

- Precise editing controls in the Arrange Inspector for fine-tuning the appearance and placement of objects.
- On-screen keypads enter exact values for text size, spacing, table size, and other parameters.
- The ability to tap or drag across objects or table cells to add or remove them from a selection.
- A preference to open documents in edit mode at all times.
- Adding phone number links to table cells, text objects, and shapes.
- When exporting your spreadsheet to Microsoft Excel, you can now choose to exclude the summary worksheet in Numbers.

Keynote for Mac has received two new updates:

- While presenting, you can now view your presenter notes, the current slide, and the next slide in a separate window.
- Thumbnail images in the build order window now make editing complex sequences easier.

Depending on how you got your Mac, you may or may not have Keynote installed. It is simple to obtain. Even better, it's completely free! The only catch is that not all Macs are supported.

Keynote is only a digital download; no physical copies are available. The file size is a few hundred megabytes.

KEYNOTE FEATURES

In the search bar, type Keynote and press the return key. If you have it, the return result will include an Open button; otherwise, it will consist of a Get button. When you click Get, you'll be asked for your Apple ID and password. If you don't already have one, make one using the directions on the screen (it's free).

When you first launch Keynote, you'll be prompted to use iCloud. This is something I suggest you do because it makes it simple to save and open documents across all devices. For instance, if you're working on a presentation on your phone, you can open that document and continue working on it from your tablet (a smooth process). If you set up iCloud, you can access and type documents directly in your browser. There is nothing else to install on your computer, which means you could technically use Keynote on a Windows computer, a Chromebook, or an Android device, and it doesn't require anything extra on your part once it's set up.

When you open Keynote, you'll see a directory box asking if you want to open an existing document or create a new one.

A template is a pre-made document into which you can insert text. These have already been assigned different styles and colors. The most basic styles (meaning you'll do most color/style customization) are black or white.

Thinking about how you'll send a presentation before making your choice is critical. Will you be presenting on a high-definition television or a smaller device?

This is significant because Keynote has two different dimensions: Standard and Wide. These two dimensions are visible at the top of the template menu. The template's styling will remain the same, but the size ratio will be slightly different. Standard is the universal format and is ideal if you are unsure how you will present. Wide is recommended for widescreen TVs; standard will result in black bars on the sides of the screen. Both will work, but it will fit better if you choose the appropriate ratio before presenting.

When using Keynote for the first time, users usually experience disappointment. You might wonder why. Assuming you use PowerPoint, you are probably accustomed to its ribbons, menus, and options. In contrast, Keynote seems to be a little lacking. You mustn't worry though, there are many possibilities if you know where to search, and I'll show you how to locate it in this book.

If you're already overwhelmed by the number of options, you can hide the side panel by clicking the Format button in the upper right corner. Hint: clicking once on any of these buttons reveals it, and clicking on it hides it.

Now that you've got a blank screen, let's go over the fundamentals of Keynote.

All Slides / Selecting All

This means selecting everything in your document. It's a very strong command! It displays the same options as Select, but any changes you make will be reflected throughout the document. To select everything, press Command + A on your keyboard.

Options

What happens after you have some content on your slide? The options box appears when you click with two fingers on your trackpad or mouse. We'll go over these options as we progress through the book.

Copy, Cut, and Paste

You can use keyboard shortcuts to copy and paste words (as well as images, tables, and charts) more quickly. Copying the content is as simple as selecting it and pressing COMMAND + C. Selecting the content and pressing COMMAND + X will suffice. Similarly, pressing COMMAND + V will copy the content wherever you want it in the document.

Find

You can find all the uses of the word you want to find from your menu bar; simply select Edit > Find > Find. You can also select Find & Replace by clicking the down arrow on the left side.

Replace and Find

Replace and Find is a useful Keynote feature that allows you to replace your selection with alternatives. Assume you've finished creating 50 slides for your big presentation on why men are mean. When you're done, however, you realize the topic isn't men being mean, but pigs being mean! You can change 'men' to 'pigs' in seconds!

From your menu bar, select Edit > Find. From here, you can find all the uses of the word you want to find, but you can also click the down arrow on the left side and select Find & Replace. This lets you search for a word (top line) and replace the word once it finds it (bottom line). When you have both the find and replace word added, you can click Replace & Find.

Look Up

Keynote includes a handy little dictionary. To see the definition of any word, select it, tap the trackpad twice to bring up the options menu, and then tap Look Up. The dictionary will provide multiple definitions (as well as a thesaurus); additionally, you can select options on the bottom to see movies related to the word, Siri Knowledge (encyclopedic information), apps related to it, and more!

Copy Style

The Copy Style command, like the Microsoft Word format painter feature, allows you to copy and paste styles. To make one piece of text look like another, select the text with the format you want to copy, click Format > Copy Style; then select the text you want to change, and click Format > Paste Style. This can save you a lot of time!

Hyperlink

Simply type out the link to insert a hyperlink to an internet resource. Keynote automatically detects hyperlinks and will insert the link for you. Simply click the link and tap Link Settings to edit or change the text displayed. You can edit the link itself, change the text displayed, or remove the link entirely from this page.

If you aren't typing a web address but want to link it to one (for example, "I go to UCLA" and provide a hyperlink to UCLA), select the word you wish to hyperlink and click with two fingers to bring up the options. Simply click Add Link and choose the type of link you want to add. You can edit and delete it in the same way that you did in the previous paragraph.

Undo/Redo

If you make a mistake (for example, deleting a paragraph that you shouldn't have deleted), you can undo it by selecting Edit > Undo; you can also redo it from the same menu.

Menus Layers

The best method to approach Keynote is through menu layers. The first layer is the slide itself, followed by the elements on that slide (i.e., text boxes, graphics, bullet points, etc.). You'll notice three menu option icons on the right side of your screen: Format, Animate, and Document.

Format

The element will be present if you slide. If you use the same type of slide over and over, this can be a huge time saver. In the Format menu, you can also change the background; for example, if you want to use a different color (or an image as the background), you can do so here.

Animate

The following menu is Animate. Animate is a slide transition; for example, when it appears, the slide will appear to fall onto the screen (or leaves). You can have this happen On Click, which means it happens as soon as you click your mouse, or you can add a timed delay after a set number of seconds or minutes. Most people will prefer on-click; using the timed feature would be ideal if you were turning your slide into a short movie.

There are dozens of different animations to experiment with. You can see a preview of them by hovering your mouse over the name and clicking preview.

When you select, a new menu with options for that animation will appear. The options will vary depending on the type of animation chosen. Most will only allow you to change the direction of the animation and how it begins (i.e., On Click). At the top, you can also change and preview the transition.

Document

The slide's final menu option is Document. You can change the theme (if you started with the wrong one) and select a different size at the bottom. For example, suppose you prepared the presentation in 4:3 but discovered on the day of the presentation that it would be shown on a widescreen display. 4:3 will still work, but black bars will appear on the sides. So, you can adjust the size here to make it more comfortable. Remember that changing the size may cause changes to the slide, such as moving text boxes and images. When changing the size of your presentation, it's always a good idea to go over it again.

In the Document menu, there is a second menu tab for audio. Most people will not use this feature, but it is an excellent tool if you want to make a movie out of your slide that people can watch later on the internet.

The elements menus aren't that dissimilar to the slide menus; in fact, many of them are identical. The most noticeable difference will be when you select a format from the menu. When you edit an element, you have three options: Style, Text, and Arrangement (some elements, such as Images, will look slightly different and not have the Text tab). You can add a border, fill, and shadow to the element under style; what I find most useful is the Opacity option. This option makes the element transparent, which is helpful if using an image behind the text.

You can change the type of text under text (a subtitle, title, or body, for example). When you click it, you'll be presented with several options. "Body" is normal text in a document—the text you're reading right now is Body Text; however, documents have several types of paragraph text.

There are options for Style, Layout, and More under this. Let's stick with style for the time being, so the next option is font. This is the font, 11pt Helvetica. If you tap on it, you'll be able to change the font and size. Keynote has a good font selection, including old standbys like Arial, Times New Roman, and Helvetica. Comic Sans (though Papyrus made the cut), Calibri, and Cambria are notable absences. The "regular" drop-down menu displays all of the font's style options (some fonts have different options).

The following three buttons are pretty standard. If you're unfamiliar with computerized word processing, remember that B stands for bold, I stands for italic, and U stands for underline. The S with a line through it inserts a strikethrough into any text you type. Your alignment buttons are located beneath this. Tap them to align your text to the left, center, or right, or to justify it. Justified text is a text that fills precisely one line. Experiment with it to see how it works. The two buttons after that are indent buttons. They can be used to indent or to move backward through indents. Finally, you can add bulleted lists and line spacing below this (if you want to double space, for example). Arrange is the final tab.

Assume you want to insert an image behind a text box. You can add an image to your slide and position it in front of the text box, then go here and click the "Back" icon to move it behind the text box. You can also lock it to prevent it from being moved by accident.

The slide menu is pretty sparse; it's useful if you have many slides and need to find them quickly or want to add slide numbers. However, for the average presentation, you are unlikely to refer to it frequently. There is something worth discussing further in this menu: collapse. What exactly is collapse? This is an organization feature. Within those slides, you can have main slides and sub slides. You can try it out by doing this:

- Add a slide (you can add a slide by clicking on the slide in front of it and pressing enter, or by right-clicking a slide and selecting New Slide).
- Move the new slide to the right with your mouse once it's been added.
- The main slide will now be indented over it.

You can do this to as many slides as you want; did you notice the arrow on the main slide? The slide will collapse if you click on it.

The Play menu is similarly sparse, but unlike the slide menu, you'll want to pay close attention to the features if you plan to present this presentation somewhere. There are three main features here:

- Play Slideshow - This command will transform your computer into a screen. This is useful if you are presenting from your computer; if you are presenting on a TV or projector, the appearance will be different.
- Record Slideshow - Recording the presentation puts it in presenter mode, allowing you to narrate it.
- Rehearse Slideshow - Rehearse appears to be the same as record, but nothing is recorded; it is in the present mode, but it is only for practice. The idea is that your presentation will appear on the TV screen as you intended, but on your computer, it will look like the presenter's view; here, you can preview your next slides, see notes, a timer, and so on—but this is all viewable to you only.

When you customize the presenter display, you'll see various options for what appears when you're in this mode.

The View Menu is where you can show and hide menus; we've covered most of them, but there's one more to mention: Notes from the Presenter. In Presenter Notes, you can add your comments, such as an outline or even the script for what you planned to say on this slide. When you present this on a TV, your audience will not see it, but you can include it in your presenter mode display.

KEYNOTE ADDRESS USING ICLOUD

Keynote can be run directly from your browser; it's great for editing, but your computer is the best option for intensive design work. To use your browser, go to iCloud.com and sign in with your Apple ID. The first screen will list everything you can do from the cloud, including Keynote. To open it, simply click it once. If you've been saving your work to the cloud, any recent documents will appear here, and you can open them by clicking on their thumbnail once. You can also create a new document by clicking the + button in the upper right corner.

This will open Keynote for iCloud. All the features covered in this book can also be found in Keynote for iCloud.

KEYNOTE 8 FOR MAC

Keynote 8 for Mac hasn't reached its pinnacle, but Apple didn't have a wish list of features to push it forward. With the simultaneous releases of Keynote for iOS, Pages (Mac and iOS), and Numbers (Mac and iOS), the most current Mac release brings it up to date.

We haven't reviewed Keynote since version 6.5.3 in 2015, so it's worth seeing what's changed. Apple continued to push development forward with incremental releases ranging from 7.0 to 7.3, restoring several missing features in 6.5.3.

A beta of collaborative real-time editing was added in version 7.0. One of the most significant changes in Version 7.1 was adding an Object List, which made creating complicated builds much easier. Selecting and ordering items in the build was a frustrating process that resulted in literal head-to-desk slamming. It's still not as good as other presentation apps, and I've spent hours moving items around to get the correct flow—but it's doable now. Navigation and text document marking up (with replies and threaded comments) improved significantly in version 7.2.

Apple added a small set of features to Keynote 8 that make it easier to move presentations between iOS and macOS. Additionally, there is more consistency with tools and expectations across both platforms' Keynote, Pages, and Numbers. Even if nothing else has changed, this should reduce friction as you work between apps and across platforms.

Image galleries are the sole newly added interactive feature; they let you insert and caption photographs in a frame that can be manually paged through or played as an auto-advance slideshow. While setting it up, you can preview it and then advance through the images while presenting or setting it to run. Creating a pseudo-slideshow through builds in version 7.3 was a pain; now, it's as simple as dragging and dropping. You can set one of three types of builds through the images for automatic or manual playback: Appear, Dissolve, and Move In. You can specify the time between images for automated playback. This is an excellent addition.

Even on a 2017 iMac, Apple Media's selection remains highly sluggish. Even though my iCloud Photo Library contains more than 37,000 pictures, they are all stored in full quality on this iMac, thus it took a while to open the selection view. If you exit Keynote, the load progress is not lost (as in Pages 7 for Mac). The media selector is a system-wide function, but it's clear how poorly optimized it is in an image-based program.

Keynote now includes donut charts, which were previously unavailable despite the many other types of charts available in this and other Apple productivity apps. As with all app updates, there are new shapes of various types that you can insert and then edit to customize. This app and all productivity apps on both platforms now support real-time collaborative editing of Keynote files shared via the Box document service.

Apple also added the ability to reduce the file size of presentations, which is useful when dragging in full-resolution images or movies that you only want to use a portion of. You can select to downscale using Apple's versions of the more effective HEIF image and HEVC video compression, as well as clip video and audio to only store the parts utilized in the file with the HEIF image and HEVC video compression. File Size Reductio. But be careful not to create a presentation that will need to run on an older Mac; it won't be able to display some file formats.

Despite adding the suite-wide image gallery feature as a slideshow option, Keynote 8 for macOS is little more than a maintenance release. Apple should take into account a strategy for strengthening its weakest components and moving forward with new modes and better methods for designing and updating interactions even though it is a mature app that is typically simple to use.

KEYNOTE FOR IOS

Keynote for iOS has always been more focused on interaction than its macOS counterpart, partly because you're more likely to present on a single screen rather than multiple monitors. This tiny update makes this clear. Keynote for iOS now has a number of new features that bring it on line with its macOS counterpart, including a similar user interface and menu options alongside Pages and Numbers on both platforms.

The Apple Pencil or your finger can be used to create drawings on iPads with Pencil support, just like in other iWork iOS apps (Pages and Numbers). With the additional bonus that Keynote for iOS can animated your drawings by essentially replaying them, this is a helpful upgrade for Keynote that makes just as much sense here as it does in Pages.

Unfortunately, the animated drawing feature is rudimentary and requires further development. You may replay the motions you did by establishing a construct for the drawing and then choosing the Line Draw option. It shows the gestures you made stroke by stroke. You can set the overall duration of the drawing, but you can't remove strokes, control their speed, rearrange or modify them. When you use the eraser to remove a portion of a drawing, that portion is removed from all frames, making the initial drawing stages appear odd. For this feature to work, you must be flawless in your original drawing, which is a tall order.

Apple oddly relies on a subset of the standard markup toolkit for drawing in Pages and Numbers, which appears inadequate in comparison to some of the more straightforward independent drawing programs. Apple should not include a full sketching environment in these apps, but I'm not sure it's robust enough to allow users to add value to their presentations.

The company also chose not to support pressure sensitivity with the Pencil, which seems odd. To select the thickness, you must instead double tap a drawing tool. This appears to disable one of the combined flagship features of the Pencil and iPad Pro without providing any benefit.

The image gallery, which also functions as a slideshow, is Keynote's other major new feature. You add the image gallery, choose images, and then, if desired, add captions (or use a single caption for the entire show). The transitions in the slideshow can be one of three types: Appears, Dissolve, or Move In. However, it doesn't seem that you can select the interval between slides for automated playback, unlike the new Keynote for macOS, making the feature somewhat pointless.

Apple now allows you to change themes in Keynote for iOS and adjust the slide size and aspect ratio of presentations for feature parity. Previously, you would have had to send the presentation to a Mac and then back to iOS to make those changes.

Donut charts, which may make your stomach rumble, are now available in Keynote and were previously one of the few common chart options missing. As with all app updates, there are new shapes of various types that you can insert and then edit to customize.

This app and all productivity apps on both platforms now support real-time collaborative editing of Keynote files shared via the Box document service.

Since there are no app-specific improvements, Keynote for iOS lacks the polish I'd expect from a release version, but all incorporating settings are available across apps and platforms. Apple should focus more on Keynote, fix the missing image gallery features already added to the Mac version, and provide more general polish. It should also push Keynote forward with better and richer interactivity, which should be expected after many years of development.

Keynote is best suited for presenters who need to work across two screens. The first is usually a projector or large monitor, and the second is a laptop or computer screen in front of the presenter. Keynote populates the second screen with various presenter tools, such as notes, thumbnails of the previous and next slides, and a timer.

Even if you have two monitors at home, you may have been frustrated in the new world of always-online meetings, professional or social. In general, full-screen app mode in macOS doesn't work well with videoconferencing tools like Google Meet, Microsoft Teams, Zoom, and others because you typically have to stay in the app that's gone full screen to keep it working in that mode.

Keynote, in particular, is difficult. In Zoom, for example, you must open the Keynote slide deck rather than enter slideshow mode (Play Slideshow). Instead, you return to Zoom, select the Keynote slide window using its screen-sharing option, then return to Keynote and begin the presentation.

Even with all that fiddling, you must remain in Keynote to present. Certain features of some conferencing tools (including Zoom) can be accessed via floating overlays. Zoom, for example, can display a resizable strip of the participants watching the session. (Keynote does provide the option to hide Keynote in presentation mode and return to the previous app without breaking out of full-screen mode by pressing H—not Command-H, but simply H.)

However, you can have more power and freedom with a new Keynote option that Apple unveiled in July, especially if you want to bounce between other applications or spend most of your time in the videoconferencing app while presenting. In my trick, that new presentation option is combined with the Keynote for iOS/iPad app.

Play Slideshow In Window, a feature added by Apple to Keynote, displays interactive slides in a regular window as opposed to the single- or dual-monitor full-screen mode that was previously necessary. The presentation window can be moved and resized. You can start the slideshow and then share its window in a videoconferencing app, eliminating the need to display the raw Keynote interface before starting the presentation, as with a full-screen slideshow.

Because the Play Slideshow In Window option is a regular window, you can switch between apps without causing Keynote problems. However, two issues remain: You must first return to the window (or go backward) to advance slides. Second, none of the tools used by the presenter are available.

This is where the mobile app comes into play. You can use the Keynote Remote feature on your iPhone or iPad to connect Keynote to your Mac.

This sequence, once paired, can be used to share a Keynote screen. The following example is for Zoom, but it applies to any tool that allows screen-sharing of a window or portion of a window:

1. Launch Keynote for macOS and open your slide deck.
2. Select Play Slideshow In Window.
3. In an active Zoom meeting on your Mac, click the Share Screen button, navigate to the Basic tab, and then select the Keynote window. Click the Share button.
4. Using Keynote Remote on your iPhone or iPad, select your Mac and tap Play (even if the presentation is already playing—this tap asserts control by the Keynote mobile app).

5. Tap the side-by-side screen icon and choose a mode that displays notes and slides as desired. You can view your notes by selecting Current And Notes, Next And Notes, or Notes Only.

CHAPTER 2: MANAGING DOCUMENTS WITH KEYNOTE

Saving in Keynote is simple—primarily if you've worked with Windows before. It's located under File > Save. Before we move on to other critical features in Keynote, I'd like to review some of the more complicated ways to manage documents.

DOCUMENT RENAMING

It is very simple to rename documents. There are several ways to accomplish this in Keynote. When your document is open, simply click on the name in the top center of the document. The next way is file> Rename.

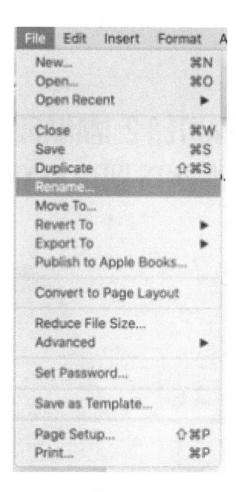

The third way is to find it in Finder, click with two fingers, and select Rename.

USING ICLOUD TO SYNC DOCUMENTS

Despite the popularity of iPhones and iPads, Apple users are frequently stranded in a Windows-based world. Although Keynote is an excellent program, it is incomprehensible to Microsoft PowerPoint. Fortunately, Keynote provides several options for sharing and exporting Keynote documents in various formats. In addition, thanks to iCloud, moving documents between Apple devices is a breeze.

If you've enabled iCloud in your Keynote app, your documents will automatically sync across all your devices with no effort. You can also access your documents online at www.icloud.com from any internet connection.

E-MAILING A KEYNOTE DOCUMENT

E-mailing documents is one of the simplest ways to share your document. Navigate to Share > Make a copy.

COLLABORATING

You can also work on a document by going to Share > Collaborate With Others.

This brings up an option asking how you would like to share the document.

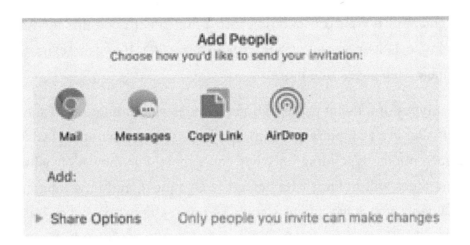

I recommend selecting the Share Options drop-down menu to ensure that the appropriate permissions are enabled. You can, for example, make the document readable to anyone you share it with or who receives it; you can also grant the user the ability to make changes.

EXPORT A KEYNOTE PRESENTATION

By default, your file will be saved as a Keynote presentation. That's great if you have Keynote, but if you want to share it (or open it) on a computer that doesn't have Keynote or create a universal PDF that anyone can see, you'll need to export it. This is relatively simple.

Navigate to File> Export. There are seven different types of files:

1. Keynote '09
2. PDF
3. PowerPoint
4. Movie
5. Animated GIF
6. Images
7. HTML

If you want to preserve all of the formatting in the document and make it look exactly like it does in Keynote, PDF is the best option. Movie and Animated GIFs are good if you stick them somewhere, like a website, and let them present themselves—in other words, the slides advance without clicking. Each slide will be exported as an Image. HTML transforms your presentation into a website.

EXPORTING A FILM

Why would you want to turn your presentation into a film? People do this for various reasons, the most prominent being to deliver presentations without a speaker. However, exporting a movie can be used for digital signage, web pages, and more.

You can export two types of moving presentations: movies and animated GIFs. An animated GIF is typically shorter, smaller in size (and resolution), and lacks sound, making it ideal for websites. You'll have a few different options depending on what you export. For movies, it will ask if it will play automatically, what slides will be in it (the default is all slides), and how long between slides and builds (i.e., the elements you have added - such as images and text boxes—assuming you have transitions applied to them); the final option is the resolution. For animated GIFs, it will inquire about the number of slides, the resolution, and the frame rate (more frame rates will typically increase your file size).

PRINTING

Go to File > Print to print a document. There's also a PDF save option at the bottom of the print menu. It is Keynote's equivalent of Print to File.

CHAPTER 3: CREATING NEW PRESENTATIONS WITH KEYNOTE

When working with a presentation app, creating new presentations seems like the logical place to start, so let's do just that, shall we? To make a new Keynote presentation (by format)

- For OS X: Select File > New or press -N to access the Theme Chooser. Choose a theme for your new presentation by clicking the Choose button in the lower right corner. Keep in mind the Standard and Wide buttons at the top of the window if you want to use a slightly different format.

- For iOS: Tap the Create Presentation icon to open the Theme Chooser from the Presentations manager (if you're already in a presentation, tap Presentations in the upper left corner). When you tap the theme you want to use, it will open automatically.

- For Apple iCloud: To open the Theme Chooser, click the Create Presentation icon from the iCloud Keynote screen. Select the theme you want to use, and then click Choose in the upper right corner of the Theme Chooser window to open it.

Presentations can be saved and renamed. Because creating presentations without saving them is ridiculous (yes, I said it), let's look at how we can save (and rename) them:

- To save a presentation in OS X, press -S or select File > Save. The Save As window will appear if you save this presentation for the first time. Simply give the presentation a title, select a location for it, and click the Save button. To rename a presentation, select File > Rename, type the new name (the presentation title in the middle of the window will be highlighted blue), and press RETURN; your presentation has now been renamed.

- For iOS: Keynote saves your presentations automatically, but it names them boringly like "Presentation" or "Presentation 2" by default, so you'll appreciate the ability to rename presentations easily. Tap the presentation name you want to rename in the Presentations manager. In the Rename Presentation screen, enter the name of your presentation in the field provided and tap Done.

- For iCloud: Keynote for iCloud saves your presentations automatically, but like iOS, you start with names like "Presentation." Fortunately, renaming the new presentation is just as simple. Open the Presentations manager, select the presentation you want to rename, type the new name into the provided field, and press RETURN.

Keynote for OS X (but not iOS or iCloud) allows you to view your presentation in four different ways, each of which is useful in different circumstances:

- **Navigator Mode (Default)**: The slide navigator on the left side of the window displays all your slides and the currently selected slide in the window. Slides can be reorganized by dragging them up and down the navigator.

- **View Only the Slideshow**: As the name implies, this view displays only the currently selected slide in the window and does not allow you to navigate to other slides.

- **View of a Light Table:** Arranges all the slides as if they were on a light table. You can quickly view and reorganize the slides by dragging and dropping them into a different order.

USING PASSWORDS AND LOCKING PRESENTATIONS

Keynote allows you to use a password to prevent those who don't know it from changing your presentation, and you can even lock it to prevent anyone from tampering with it.

A password protects your presentation from spies, other nefarious characters, and innocent bystanders who might accidentally change its contents. When a password is assigned to a presentation, no one can open it, let alone change it, unless they know the password.

To give a password to a presentation, do the following:

- For OS X: select File > Set Password to open the password dialog. Enter the password in the Password and Verify fields, optionally enter a hint in the Password Hint field (Apple recommends it, but I don't), and click the Set Password button.
- For iOS: Open the presentation, then select Tools > Set Password. Enter the password in the Password and Verify fields, add a hint in the Password Hint field if desired (Apple suggests it, but I'm not sure why), and tap the Go button on the on-screen keyboard. Even if you don't enter a hint, you must tap the Hint field before the blue Go button appears.
- For Apple iCloud: Open the presentation, click the Tools icon, and set a password. Enter the password in the Password and Verify fields, optionally enter a hint in the Password Hint field (Apple recommends it, but why?), and then click the Set Password button. Simply type the password when prompted to open a password-protected presentation; you're up a creek without a paddle if you don't know the password.

LOCKING PRESENTATIONS

When you lock a presentation, no one can edit, rename, move, or delete it. However, you should know that locking a presentation is only available in the OS X version of Keynote. To finish a presentation:

1. Move the mouse pointer over the presentation title (which must be open in Keynote to be locked) until you see a small gray arrow next to it; click the gray arrow.
2. To lock the presentation, check the Locked box. To return to the presentation, click outside the window. When you try to change a presentation element, you will be reminded that it is locked.

TRANSFERRING PRESENTATIONS TO AND FROM ICLOUD

Moving your presentations to iCloud makes them available to you and others from any computer or iOS device that can connect to the internet. Moving presentations away from iCloud has the opposite effect, so proceed cautiously.

To transfer a presentation from your computer to iCloud, follow these steps:

1. Select File > Move To.
2. From the pop-up menu, choose a location. If you don't see the location you're looking for in the menu, select Other at the bottom to browse your hard drive.

3. Select the Move option. Your presentation will be physically moved from its previous location to the one you specify, rather than copied. This feature is only available in the Mac version of Keynote.

USING ICLOUD TO SHARE PRESENTATIONS

Keynote allows you to share an iCloud presentation with anyone by sending them a link to the presentation.

When you share a presentation via iCloud, you send a web link to the location of the presentation within iCloud. Anyone with Keynote (on a Mac, an iOS device, or a Windows PC using iCloud) can open (and Edit) the presentation, and any changes they make will be saved to it, so be cautious about who you share it with. The links can be delivered to your intended recipient via e-mail, Messages, Twitter, Facebook, or any other method you can think of.

To share a presentation from OS X via iCloud Keynote:

1. Start by opening the presentation you want to share. Protect the presentation with a password if you haven't already done so!
2. In the toolbar, click the Share button.
3. Using the Share Link Via iCloud context menu, choose the method you want to use to share the iCloud link to your presentation. When the link is sent to the recipient(s), the Share icon in the toolbar changes from a white box with an upward arrow to a couple of green-colored people, indicating that the presentation has been shared. When in shared mode, click the Share button to do the following:
   - Use the Change Password button to change the password for the presentation.
   - Click the Stop Sharing button to stop sharing the presentation.
   - Send the link to someone else by selecting a method from the pop-up menu and clicking the Send Link button.
   - Move your mouse pointer over the link until you see a gray button labeled Copy Link, click it to copy the link to your Mac's clipboard, and then paste it into any presentation or other sharing mechanism you prefer.

To share a presentation via iCloud from iOS, follow these steps:

1. Launch the presentation you want to share (and please password-protect it).
2. In the toolbar, tap the Share button.

3. Select the option to Share Link Via iCloud. Choose how you want to share the iCloud link to your presentation. You'll notice that another method of sharing that can be used from an iOS device to share the link with other iOS devices is AirDrop.

As in OS X, the Share icon has been replaced by a couple of green guys, indicating that the presentation is in shared mode. When in shared mode, tap the Share button and then the Share Settings option to do the following:

- Change the presentation password by tapping Change password.
- Stop sharing the presentation by tapping the Stop Sharing button.
- Tap Send link and choose a method from the pop-up menu to send the link to someone else.
- Tap the link to bring up a dark gray button labeled copy; tap the Copy button to copy the link to your device's clipboard, and then paste the link into any notification or sharing mechanism you prefer.

To share a presentation via iCloud from within Keynote for iCloud, follow these steps:

1. Open the presentation you want to share (it's password-protected, right?)
2. In the toolbar, click the Share button, then the blue Share Presentation button.
3. A window appears with the text "This presentation has been shared."

You can do the following from within this window:

- Using the Change Password button, change the password for the presentation (or add a password by using the Add Password button).
- Click the Stop Sharing button to stop sharing the presentation.
- Click the E-mail Link button in the iCloud Mail app to send the link to someone else.
- Highlight the link by pressing -C (Mac) or CONTROL-C (PC), then copy the link to your computer's clipboard and paste it into any presentation or sharing mechanism you like. To open the "This presentation is shared" window again, click the Share button in the toolbar (the green people are back!), and then click Settings.

CHAPTER 4: WORKING WITH PHOTOS IN KEYNOTE

INSERT IMAGE

There are several methods for inserting an image. You can copy and paste an image, drag a photo into the document, or manually select it. To manually select it, go to Insert > Choose and then locate the file location. However, adding a photo from the menu is the quickest way. Click the image button to see all the different types of media you can add. You can get photos by clicking on Photos or Image Gallery (if the photos are in your gallery) or clicking "Choose" to select the photo's location.

If you select photos, it will show you only the photos in your Mac's photos, not all of your photos. You could have a photo on your USB drive, for example. If that's the case, select "Choose" from the previous menu instead of photos.

ROTATE AND RESIZE

After you've inserted your image, you can move, resize, and rotate it with your mouse. Resizing is a simple process. Click the image, then move to the image's corner or side and drag the little squares on the edges in and out. To rotate the image, repeat the process, but when you reach the image's corner, press the Command key on your keyboard. This will display a curved line as well as the percentage of rotation as you move the image.

Looking for pictures? When you click on the image, you'll notice that the text-formatting side panel has changed. There is now a new menu with image formatting controls. The top of this menu has three buttons (Style, Image, and Arrange); we'll go over the first one in the next section, but for now, select Arrange. There's a section at the bottom of this menu called Rotate; Angle is what you want to use. The mouse is a quick and easy way to rotate your image, but it is not the most precise method. In addition to the Angle, you can use the arrows to flip the image vertically and horizontally.

PLACEMENT

Because a photo is essentially just a layer in your slide, you can put it in front of or behind other layers. You'll notice a back / front icon bar on the Arrange menu. This is where you can move the image behind or in front of other images.

IMAGE GROUP

Arrange has one more section that is greyed out: Grouping. Grouping is greyed out because it requires two images to be used. Add another image, click one, press command on your keyboard, and select the second image; the Group option is no longer greyed out. Grouping combines two images so that when you edit the size, rotation, and so on, you treat the two photos as if they were one. You do not need to ungroup an image if you only want to edit it. You can double-click the image to tell Keynote that you want to keep them grouped but only make changes to one of them.

WATERMARK

The simplest way to create a Watermark in Keynote is to move the image behind everything and make it slightly transparent in the Style menu. But what if you want the same image on every slide? As mentioned in the previous chapter, you can accomplish this by modifying the master slides.

MASK AND ALPHA EDITING

Select the Image button with your image selected (note: if the images are grouped, you must double-click the image you want to edit—you cannot edit both images simultaneously). This displays image enhancement options. The Adjustments section is at the bottom; this section is self-explanatory - the Exposure and Saturation sliders will change the amount of exposure/saturation in the image. The Enhance button will automatically enhance the image based on what the computer thinks it should look like (the reset button will undo it). A control button next to the Enhance button brings up additional adjustment controls. Most people are unlikely to require this many controls, but knowing they are available is helpful.

The top section, Edit Mask and Instant Alpha, may be more challenging to understand. Edit Mask is essentially a cropping tool for images. You can use this to remove portions of an image without resizing it. Instant Alpha is one of my favorite image editing programs. It removes the image's background. It's ideal when your image has a very solid background.

When you click it, the cursor changes to a square box, allowing you to click and drag over the areas you want to remove. As you click, the removed sections will change color to indicate what has been removed. When you're finished, release the mouse, and click the done button.

When you remove the background, it also auto crops; for example, if you remove the background from the top, the image is automatically cropped to accommodate it.

IMAGE ENHANCEMENT

Basic Designs

The top box allows you to quickly apply pre-defined image styles to your image. For instance, if you want a box around your image. Most people want to edit the photo manually, but if you use the arrow in this section, you'll notice a + button. After making manual changes to the image (adding transparency, borders, and so on), you can use this button to save these changes to apply them to another photo with a similar look and feel.

Border

The following section is the border; the image does not have a border by default. When you click the box with the red diagonal line, a drop-down menu with all the different styles appears. Once you've decided on a border style, you can adjust the border's weight with the slider. When you click the border preview, you will see all the different border styles for your chosen style. Styles differ depending on the style you use.

Shadows

Shadows can add dimension to your photo and make it stand out more on the page. It works similarly to Borders in that you click the thumbnail with the red line through it and then select the shadow style. When you select a style, you'll be given several shadow options for increasing or decreasing the amount of shadowing used. As you make changes, the image will update in real-time, allowing you to see the results immediately.

Reflection

Reflection is a simple check/uncheck box; you can adjust the amount of reflection using the slider, but that is the only Edit available. In the example below, you can see how the reflection gave the image the appearance of an image reflecting on the page.

Transparency

Transparency is the last style change. Transparency improves the visibility of an image.

CHAPTER 5: WORKING WITH TABLES IN KEYNOTE

Keynote integrates well with other iWork apps such as Numbers and Pages, especially regarding tables. You can manually insert tables into your document, but you can also import tables from Numbers. This section will show you how and briefly overview Numbers for the iPad.

ADDING A TABLE

If you've ever added a table in Word, you're probably used to select the size and width before adding it. In Keynote, however, you add the table and adjust it.

Tap the Table button in the top menu bar to add a table (you can also use Insert > Table from the menu options at the top of macOS). You'll have several styles to choose from, but this isn't like Word, where you can drag to the number of rows and columns you want.

INSERTING COLUMNS AND ROWS

Your table has now been inserted, but it is most likely not the correct size. A circle with two lines appears at the bottom of the last row (or side of the previous column). Click on either of those to change the number of columns/rows. You can choose by using the up and down arrows or by clicking the number and then typing the amount you want.

WORKING WITH TABLES

Working with a table in Keynote can be challenging at first. When you double-click a cell, the keyboard appears, but when you single-click it, the entire cell is selected (Microsoft Excel users should have an easier time with this concept). If there is no text, you can single-click and begin typing; however, if you want to edit the text that is already there, you must double-click.

OPTIONS FOR ROWS AND COLUMNS

To delete or add a row or column, go to the row or column you want to change and click the drop-down arrow. Several options will be presented. You can also select all by clicking the number associated with the row/column. This is useful for copying and pasting a row or column.

TABLES FOR STYLING

Apple's pre-defined tables are beautiful, but if you have a specific color scheme or style, you can easily customize your tables to match. Simply select your table (or specific cells within your table) and look to the right-side menu, which has been transformed into a table-style menu.

The first set of options applies to the whole table. All of these options would alter everything in the table. For example, you can see grids and alternating row colors in the table outline (if you want row 1 white, row 2 black, row 3 white, row 4 black, etc.). You can also change the font size and insert new rows and columns. The Table Styles at the top are pre-defined styles, similar to the image styles.

The table options are fantastic if you want to change everything about the table. But what if you only want to modify a single cell, column, or row? This is where the Cell Option tab comes in. It says "Cell," but cell here refers to anything you highlight. So, if you highlight one cell, it only highlights that cell; if you highlight multiple cells, it highlights each of those cells. What does it mean when you can change what is inside the cell in Data Format? Let's say one of your columns only contained currency; you could highlight that column and then declare that everything in those cells was currency so that a dollar sign would be appended to all the numbers in the cells.

Under Fill, you can change the color of the cell; under the border, you can change the border style, color, and weight. Conditional Highlighting is a little more subtle than the first two options.

TEXT FORMATTING OPTIONS

You should now understand how to format text. It's the same when you're doing a table. The same rules apply as before—any cell you highlight will have the text changed—so if you highlight the entire row, all the text in those cells changes. One box should be mentioned: Text in the cell should be wrapped. It's just a check/uncheck box, but it's important because if you have a long string of text and want it to fit within a cell without spilling over into the next cell, you must allow it to wrap.

Arrange Options are nearly identical to the options covered in Photo Arrangement Options, just as text options are the same as formatting options outside the table.

TABLES IMPORTING

There are several methods for importing a table from another location. The first and simplest method is to copy and paste the table. The obvious way is to use Command V, but you can also use the Edit menu. Have you noticed that there's a Paste and a Paste and Match Styles?

If you aren't getting the paste results you want, try this Paste instead.

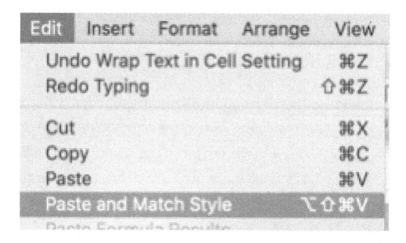

If you don't need to make changes to the table, what a lot of people prefer to do is just make a screenshot of the spreadsheet: Command + Shift + 3 (or Command + Shift + 4 if you want to do only select areas of the screen).

CHAPTER 6: WORKING WITH CHARTS IN KEYNOTE

Charts can help you present data more clearly by adding color to your documents. Keynote includes a robust Charts feature that allows you to quickly create visually appealing, customizable charts that stand out on the page. Using Charts will be a breeze now that you know how to use Tables.

ADDING A CHART

In Keynote, press the Insert button, then select Charts. You can select the chart type (bar, area, line, or pie) and the style. Choose from various color schemes in 2D, 3D, and interactive modes.

If you change your mind about your chart choice, you can always change it later without losing any data you've entered. Just tap on your favorite chart to insert it into your document.

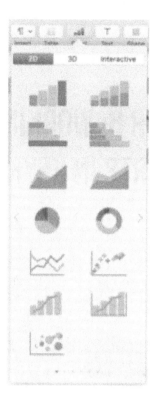

As with almost everything in Keynote, you can add Charts from the top menu (Insert > Chart).

DESIGNING YOUR PIE CHART

Once you've gathered the necessary information, it's time to style it. Using a pie chart, you'll notice three options on the side (Chart, Wedges, Arrange). Other charts, such as bar charts, have four (Chart, Axis, Series, Arrange).

The chart has no title by default, but if you check the box, a title (cleverly named "Title") is added to your chart; you'll probably want to rename it. To do so, double-click on it and begin typing (this also applies to renaming anything else in your chart). You can change the font and chart colors directly beneath the title. You will be presented with many pre-defined colors when you click on the chart. What if you want to choose your own?

There is one more minor step to selecting your colors. Double-click the wedge you want to change the color of, and then click style on the menu options to the right (A style is a new option that appears only if you double-click the wedge). Under "Fill," you can select a color. While we're in this section, let's look at Stroke and Shadow. Both of these options make a wedge stand out. This is useful if you want to show one area of the chart compared to others.

Try separating the wedge from the chart if you want it to stand out. You can select the Wedge option and adjust the Wedge Position. Consider the following example: the wedge is now separated in the chart. Let's return to the chart section and look at the other options we have for the entire chart. You can change the Chart Type, add a background, and add a shadow to it. You can change it to a different Pie chart or a line chart.

What happens if you don't double-click the wedge and change it? The wedges appear all separate. If that's what you're looking for, great! If you don't want that, undo and then double-click the wedge you want to separate. By checking the box next to Data Point Names, the names of the values will be displayed in the chart.

The values on the chart are currently displayed as a percentage; if you prefer to see them as a number (or another value type), change the Value Format setting. You probably won't notice a difference if you check Lender Lines; to see what the lines are, click the Straight drop-down and change it to Angled.

You should now see lines on the chart's side. You should be familiar with the arrange option. The same features you've seen in the Tables and Photos sections.

DESIGNING YOUR BAR CHART

You'll have no trouble styling a Bar Chart now that you've learned how to style a Pie Chart; it's the same but with more label options. You can toggle the visibility of category labels, series names, gridlines, and titles in the axis sub-tab. Similarly, you can toggle value labels, gridlines, and titles on and off in the Y-axis or X-axis sub-tabs. You can also specify the number format and adjust the value scale settings here.

Number formatting includes the option to add prefixes and suffixes, like currency symbols, or suffixes like %, millions, etc.

WORKING WITH TEMPLATES IN KEYNOTE

Keynote includes many templates. A template is a pre-formatted document that includes text and images.

The templates in Keynote are lovely, but after a while, you'll probably want a few more; if you reach that point, there are websites (and even apps) that sell Keynote templates (sometimes they are free). A simple web search for "Keynote templates" or "free Keynote templates" will demonstrate what I mean. A word of caution: use at your own risk, as with anything you download. If a website appears shady, avoid downloading a template.

To use a template like this, go to the website, find a template you like, download it to your computer's hard drive, and then sync it with your iPad, as if it were any other Keynote document, using the iTunes File Sharing syncing process described in "Basic Features." After that, Keynote will open the template, and you will be able to begin editing it. It is strongly advised that you duplicate your template document before you begin working on it so that you can keep a blank one for later use if necessary. These third-party templates are great for more variety, such as if you want to add some flair to your resume.

Keynote does not currently allow you to save templates in the Create New Document screen. However, you can get around this glaring omission by saving your "template" as a regular Keynote document.

CHAPTER 7: EXPORTING AND IMPORTING PRESENTATIONS WITH KEYNOTE

Exporting a presentation from Keynote has two implications. One is to save the file in a format other than its native.key format. The second is that the term export in Keynote refers to transferring files from an iOS device to a computer via iTunes. When working in Keynote, importing presentations is usually as simple as opening them. Importing presentations, like exporting, involves transferring files from iTunes to your iOS device.

EXPORTING KEYNOTE FILES

Keynote can export files to various formats, allowing them to be viewed and worked with in other applications.

To export a Keynote presentation within the Presentations manager and within an open presentation for Mac:

1. Start by opening the presentation you want to export.
2. Go to the File menu and hover your mouse over the Export To menu.
3. Choose the format in which you want to save your file.
4. When the Export Your Presentation dialog appears, make any necessary selections based on your exporting format.
5. Select Next.
6. Select a location to save your new file, rename it if desired, and click Export.

To export from an open presentation, do the following:

1. Navigate to Tools > Download A Copy.
2. Choose the format in which you want to save your file.
3. After formatting the presentation, Keynote will download it to your browser's default downloads folder.

To export from the Presentations manager, follow these steps:

1. Highlight the presentation you want to export by clicking once.
2. At the top of the window, click the Presentation And Sort Options button (it looks like a gear) and select Download Presentation from the menu.
3. Select the format to which you want to export your file.
4. After formatting the presentation, Keynote will download it to your browser's default downloads folder.

ADDING FILES TO KEYNOTE

Keynote supports non-native file formats such as Keynote '09 and PowerPoint. Opening a file in Keynote for OS X is the same as importing it. To open a presentation file in Keynote for OS X, follow these steps:

1. Press -O or select File > Open.
2. In the upper left corner of the window, choose iCloud or On My Mac, depending on where the presentation is located.
3. Double-click the presentation you want to open, then click the Open button in the window's lower right corner. You can also open a presentation by double-clicking it within the window.

Opening a presentation file in Keynote for iCloud is also simple. The most straightforward method is to drag and drop the file into the Presentations manager (using a supported browser, of course), but you can also upload a file:

1. Select Upload Presentation from the Settings menu (it looks like a gear).
2. Navigate to your computer and select the file you want to open. To open a presentation file in Keynote for iOS, you must first transfer the file to the device, which is where iTunes comes in.

FILE TRANSFER TO AND FROM KEYNOTE USING ITUNES

iTunes can transfer files to and from Keynote on iOS devices. This is especially helpful if you don't use or have access to iCloud but need to work on your presentations on a computer. To transfer files from iTunes to Keynote for iOS, follow these steps:

1. Connect your iOS device to your computer and launch iTunes (not the iOS device).
2. Once your device appears in the upper right corner of the window, select it in iTunes.
3. Select Apps from the toolbar at the top of the window, then scroll to the bottom.
4. Select Keynote from the Apps list in the File Sharing section.
5. Click the Add button in the lower right and then navigate to the file you want to transfer on your computer. When you've found it, select it, and then click Add. The file will appear in the Keynote Documents folder.
6. Launch Keynote from your iOS device.
7. Navigate to the Presentations manager and click the + button in the upper left corner; then select copy From iTunes. When the copy From the iTunes window appears, tap the presentation name you want to import into Keynote on your iOS device. When the transfer is finished, the presentation will appear in the Presentations manager and can be opened with a single tap.

To transfer files from Keynote for iOS to iTunes, follow these steps:

1. Connect your iOS device to your computer and launch iTunes (not the iOS device).
2. Once it appears, select your device in iTunes (it will appear in the upper right corner of the window).
3. Select Apps from the toolbar at the top of the window, then scroll to the bottom.
4. Select Keynote from the Apps list in the File Sharing section.
5. Launch Keynote on your iOS device and perform one of the following actions:
   - If the presentation you want to transfer isn't open, tap the Share button in the upper left corner of the screen (it looks like a square with an upward-pointing arrow) and then choose to Send A Copy from the menu. To highlight the presentation you want to transfer, tap it.
   - While working on the presentation you want to transfer, tap the Share button in the upper right corner of the screen and choose to Send A Copy from the menu.

6. Open the Send To iTunes window by tapping the iTunes icon.
7. Select the presentation file format from the list.

Once the transfer is complete, the presentation will appear in the Keynote Documents list on iTunes. Select the file, click the Save To button in the lower right, select a location to save the file on your computer, and click the Save To button.

CHAPTER 8: WORKING WITH SHAPES IN KEYNOTE

Shapes can be helpful additions to a document because they can draw attention to a specific area of the document or illustrate your points graphically. Keynote includes some good pre-made shapes you can use, and I'll show you how to make the most of them.

ADDING A SHAPE

Click the shape button or select Insert > Shape from the top menu to insert a shape into a document.

This will bring up all of the shapes available for you. Find the one you like and click it to insert it.

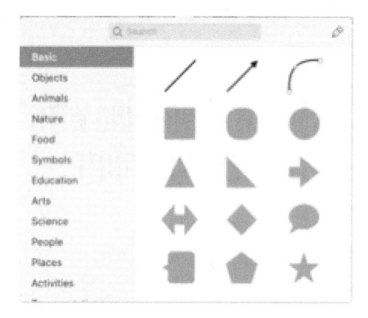

Remember that you can later change the color, border, and shadow/reflection effects! Shapes sound a little deceptive. If you're anything like me, you're probably thinking square, circle, etc. However, shapes in Keynote are similar to clipart. Yes, there are basic shapes, but there are also other things. I searched for "Dog" in the following example and received five results.

ADJUSTING PROPORTIONS AND RESIZING SHAPES

Shape resizing is similar to photo resizing: tap on a corner and drag it to the desired size. Shapes, on the other hand, allow you to change proportions. What does this imply? It's better to see than to explain.

Double tap your trackpad on the shape to bring up the shape options. Now, choose "Make Editable." The shape now has a slew of dots on it. These are the points where you can make changes. For example, consider what happened when I moved the point inward from the dog's stomach. By default, these changes are made with a curved point, but you can change this by bringing up the options again. Have you noticed the three distinct points?

SHAPES THAT MOVE AND ROTATE

Simply tap and drag a shape to a new location to move it. To rotate a shape, click the image and then the command button, just as you would an image.

Including text in a Shape To add text to a shape, double tap it to open its text field. Then simply type your text!

MAKING TEXT BOXES

There is one more type of shape, but it is not classified as such. This is a Text Box. Text Boxes are exactly what they sound like: floating text boxes.

Why should you use a Text Box instead of typing the text? You should ideally use them when creating something like a title, not when typing out your epic novel. You want to stand out with short text.

Text Boxes, unlike standard text, are treated similarly to images, allowing you to easily move them around and have other things wrap around them.

To get started, click the T in the menu.

You can also do Insert > Text Box.

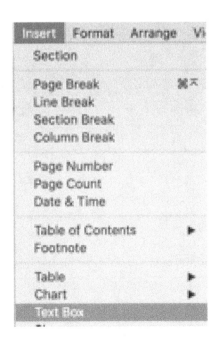

This puts a floating box with generic text in your document.

You can change the color of the box and more by clicking on style; it has all the same types of options that you'd find in the Image or Shape options.

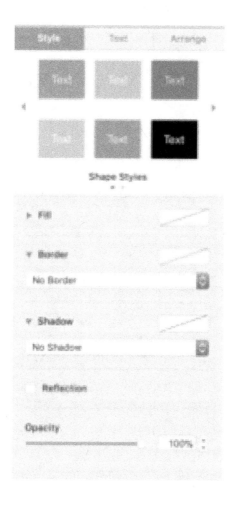

CHAPTER 9: PRINTING A PRESENTATION

PRINTING FROM MAC OS X

To print Keynote presentations for OS X, press -P or select File > Print to open the Print dialog sheet, and then do the following:

1. In the Printer pop-up menu, choose the printer to which you want to send the print job.

2. Make any other changes you think are necessary, such as changing the number of copies to Print or specifying two-sided printing (if your printer supports such a feature). Click the Keynote pop-up menu and select Page Attributes from the options to see options such as Paper Size.

3. To send your job to the printer, click the Print button in the lower right corner.

USING IOS TO PRINT

Printing from Keynote in iOS is a breeze. To do this, follow these steps:

1. Start by opening the presentation you want to print.

2. Tap the Tools icon in the upper right corner, then select Print from the menu.

3. Tap Next after selecting the layout options you want to use.

4. If the printer you require isn't already selected, tap Select Printer. Explore the available printers and tap to choose the one you want to use.

5. Select how many copies of the presentation you want to print and press the + or - button.

6. Select Print to send your job to the printer. Go to the printer and reap the benefits of your efforts.

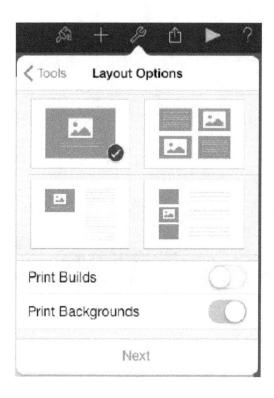

USING ICLOUD TO PRINT

Keynote for iCloud printing differs from Keynote for OS X or iOS printing because Keynote for iCloud can only print PDFs. Furthermore, Keynote PDFs will print directly from your browser or your computer's default PDF application rather than from Keynote itself. To print from iCloud, go to:

1. Launch the presentation you want to print.

2. Select Print from the Tools menu in the upper right corner.

3. Keynote will create a PDF version of your presentation. When the PDF is ready, click the Open PDF button to open it in your browser or your preferred PDF application. The PDF generation process can take a long time if your presentation contains many slides.

4. Print normally from your browser or a PDF app.

CHAPTER 10: ENHANCING A PRESENTATION WITH KEYNOTE

ADDING VIDEO TO A SLIDE

Create a new slide, then select Movies from your Photos library or Movies folder by clicking Media in the toolbar. Drag a video onto the slide. Drag the corner handles to resize them.

Choose whether the movie should play automatically or when clicked in the Format inspector's Movie tab and whether it should loop. Trim the excess at the beginning or end of the video. When the movie is not playing, use the Poster Frame slider to select what is displayed.

INCLUDE OBJECT LINKS

Web and e-mail addresses in the text are converted to links automatically. (You can disable this in Keynote's preferences, under Auto-Correction > Formatting.)

To add a link to an image, shape, video, or another object, hold down the Ctrl key and select Add Link. You must type or paste an address for the Webpage and E-mail options.

The ability to jump to a slide is helpful for kiosk displays, app and website prototypes, and kid-friendly interactive adventures.

HOW TO APPLY MAGIC MOVE

Select and Duplicate

Magic Move is a tool for animating object movement between slides. Make a slide. To duplicate it, select it in the slide navigator and press Cmd+D. Remove any elements you don't want on the copy and replace them with new ones.

Change and Organize

On the second slide, reposition the elements that you want to animate. You can also animate the rotation and size of the slides between them. When you're finished, select the first slide, and press the Animate button on the toolbar.

Personalize the Effect

Select Magic Move from the 'Add an Effect' menu. Customize the animation's duration, acceleration (abruptness of start and end), what starts, how text morphs, and whether unwanted objects disappear instantly or gradually fade in the sidebar.

Use Objects and Media in Your Presentations

Text within your slides should be formatted. Use tables to convey information concisely. Add charts to your information to make it more visually appealing. Some presentations require only the bare essentials, such as titles and bullet points, to convey their message. Most people understand, however, that adding some spice to a presentation, such as cool images and highly stylized text, can get an audience's juices flowing and turn great information into phenomenal information.

ADDING OBJECTS AND MEDIA TO SLIDES

Media such as images and video, as well as objects such as shapes, can transform a presentation from good to WOW in just a few mouse clicks or screen taps. Keynote is aware of this fact and is ready and willing to assist you in making your presentations pop, or better yet.

Image Insertion

Themes are a great place to start when creating a presentation; most include image placeholders just waiting for you to replace them with your own. While Keynote themes make it extremely easy to insert images into slides, you don't have to use them every time you create a presentation. You can begin with a blank slide and insert images wherever you want.

Adding images to slides in any version of Keynote, with or without a placeholder, is a breeze. Remember that a placeholder is just an idea; a good page design expert at Apple created the theme and placeholders to inspire you to create your slide. You are not required to keep the images in the same locations or even at the same sizes as they were in the original unaltered theme.

When working in Keynote for OS X, there are four simple ways to insert images into your slides:

1. Simply drop an image from the Finder into your slide.
2. Select Choose from the Insert menu, browse your Mac for the image you want, and click Insert.
3. Click the image button in the lower right corner of an image placeholder (which looks like an illustration of a mountain and the sun) and select an image from your iPhoto or Aperture library.
4. In the toolbar, click the Media button and select an image from your iPhoto or Aperture library.

Adding images to Keynote for iOS is straightforward:

1. Tap + in the toolbar, click the Media tab, or click + in an image placeholder (lower right corner).
2. Select an image by tapping it; Keynote only displays images stored on your device.

To add an image to a slide in Keynote for iCloud, do one of the following:

1. Drag an image from the Finder (or your desktop if you're using a PC) into the slide.
2. In the toolbar, click the Image button, then the Choose Image button, browse your computer for the desired image, and then click Choose.

Cropping Images

When you mask an image, you hide parts of the image that you don't want to be visible in your slide while leaving the rest of the image intact. In all three versions of Keynote, the following steps are taken:

1. Double-click (or double tap on iOS) the image you want to mask to reveal the masking controls. The default mask is set to the size of your original image.
2. To mask your image, do one of the following:
   - To resize the image, drag the slider.
   - Drag the image within the mask window to reposition it.
   - To move the mask, drag its border.
   - To resize the mask, drag its handles.
4. When you're finished masking the image, click or tap Done.

Removing Image Elements

The Instant Alpha tool in Keynote for OS X or iOS (I'm afraid iCloud isn't a part of the fun of this feature) can help you hide parts of an image that you don't want to populate your slide. No need to be concerned because Instant Alpha doesn't mess with the original image.

To use Instant Alpha in Keynote for OS X, follow these steps:

1. Select the image by clicking on it.
2. In the Format bar's Image tab, click the Instant Alpha button.
3. Locate the color you want to remove from the image using the targeting tool (it looks like a square with crosshairs).
4. Begin removing the selected color from your image by clicking. Drag to remove more color (and those surrounding it). Holding down the OPTION key while dragging will instantly remove all instances of the color from the image. Holding the SHIFT key while dragging will restore the colors to your image.
5. When finished, click Done.

To use Instant Alpha in Keynote for iOS, follow these steps:

1. Choose an image.
2. In the toolbar, select the Format inspector (paintbrush) icon.
3. Select image, then Instant Alpha.
4. Drag your finger over the area (or color) of the image you want to remove. The more you drag, the more the colors are removed.
5. When finished, tap Done.

Adding and Removing Shapes

Shapes, such as boxes, circles, and lines, enhance your slides more subtly than images, but the effect can be just as powerful. Keynote allows you to use as many shapes as you want and has a large selection. If that isn't enough, you can even draw your shape if what you're looking for isn't available in Keynote (OS X only, though).

Each Keynote version can add shapes, so let's look at them individually.

To insert a shape into Keynote for Mac:

1. In the toolbar, click the Shape button.
2. Click to select a shape from the pop-up menu. To scroll through all the options, click the gray dots at the bottom of the left and right arrows on either side of the menu.
3. Drag the shape around your slide by clicking and dragging it.
4. To change the shape's size, click and drag the handles around it.

To add a shape in Keynote for iOS, follow these steps:

1. In the toolbar, press the + button.
2. Press the Shape button (it looks like a square). To see more shapes in the menu, swipe left or right.
3. Tap on a shape to insert it into your slide.
4. Drag the shape to the position in your slide that you want it to be.
5. Drag the handles to change the shape's size.

To add a shape in Keynote for iCloud, follow these steps:

1. In the toolbar, click the Shape button.
2. Drag the shape into position within the slide by clicking and dragging it.
3. Change the color and other attributes of the shape using the options in the Shape tab of the format panel (right side of the window).

Textualizing Shapes

You can add text inside a shape in Keynote for OS X and iOS (but not iCloud as of this writing). This is similar to adding text to a text box, except instead of a square, you can type in any shape you want. To add text to a shape in Keynote for Mac or iOS, follow these steps:

1. Select the shape by double-clicking (OS X) or double tapping (iOS).
2. Once the cursor appears inside the shape, begin typing your text. If your text does not fit the shape, drag the selection handles to trim it, change the font size, or resize the shape.

Changing the Curves of a Shape

Keynote for OS X allows you to edit an image's curves using sharp or curved lines and create unique and interesting shapes. To edit a shape's curves in Keynote for Mac:

1. In your slide, select the shape.
2. Select Make Editable from the list under Format > Shapes, And Lines (not the Format button in the toolbar).
3. Drag the handles that appear on the edges of your shape to create whatever shape you want. To change the type of line produced by a handle, double-click it: A square handle indicates that the handle produces sharp (straight) lines; a circle handle suggests that the handle makes curved lines.
4. When you're finished editing the curves, click outside the shape.

CONCLUSION

Thank you for reading this book. Keynote is Apple's presentation tool, similar to PowerPoint in Microsoft Office. However, because it supports rich media such as audio and video, it can do much more than just create slides. You can use it to make standalone animations, interactive projects, and even mock-up websites and apps, though you'll need to import frame templates.

Keynote allows you to record audio, which is helpful if you want to record a narration track. Both video and audio can be set to start automatically when a mouse or trackpad is clicked or to loop continuously while the slide containing it is on-screen.

Click Keynote Live in the app's toolbar to give a presentation over the internet or a local network. While inviting people, you can also set a password.

Keynote is, like Microsoft PowerPoint, a solution for creating eye-catching presentations. For many years, PowerPoint was the industry standard for apps used to create presentations, but since Keynote's release, many presenters have become interested in it. Keynote began as software by Apple co-founder Steve Jobs to create his world-famous Macworld Expo keynote address presentations. It was eventually made available to the general public in January 2003.

Keynote, an app from the iWork family, executes tasks with the same grace, efficiency, and strength as its word processor and spreadsheet siblings. If you've worked with PowerPoint to create presentations, you'll feel at home with Keynote.

Good luck!

www.ingramcontent.com/pod-product-compliance
Lightning Source LLC
LaVergne TN
LVHW060141070326

832902LV00018B/2888